~IVES WASHBURN · PUBLISHER · NEW YORK~

D1108303

TIMES SQUARE
TINTYPES

TIMES SQUARE TINTYPES

BEING TYPEWRITER CARICATURES OF
THOSE WHO MADE THEIR NAMES
ALONG THE NOT SO STRAIGHT AND
VERY NARROW PATH OF BROADWAY

By

SIDNEY SKOLSKY

Illustrated by
GARD

NEW YORK   MCMXXX
IVES WASHBURN · PUBLISHER

PRINTED IN THE UNITED STATES OF AMERICA
BY THE VAIL-BALLOU PRESS, INC., BINGHAMTON, N. Y.

To
KEATS SPEED

"Broadway's a great street when you're going up. When you're going down—take Sixth Avenue."

WM. ANTHONY McGUIRE

INTRODUCTION

I am not here to introduce Mr. Skolsky, the author of these subsequent sketches. Like all true biographers, Mr. Skolsky has a passion for self-effacement. He will hiss me for disclosing him in even the most general terms.

It is my theory that all good Broadway columnists—a race apart—are small of frame, soft of voice, racy with all the sophistication of the naïve-at-heart, with eyes that are incurably big with the wonder and glee of what they see in that fabulous district, the vicinity of Times Square. Mr. Skolsky is a favorite Broadway columnist, and he looks his likable part.

On *The Sun*, we used to leave Mr. Skolsky to his own sly devices. It would be better fun to wait and see what new personality he'd choose to lightning-sketch and pin up on the New York sky line each succeeding week. He was—still is, in his new-found quarters on *The News*—inexhaustible about that business. His world brims over with possibilities for his peculiar sort of portraiture. His asylum of the great and the near-great will never run empty. He will always, I'm sure, greet every up-and-coming understudy with her literary tintype before she is six paces on her way to stardom.

The charcoal with which Mr. Skolsky draws is a native product. It can be made out of nothing else than Broadway's compressed soot. And he wields it with a hand grown exceedingly quick and sure in the nervous racket of Broadway crowds. His wit has the telegraphic tempo which insures clean and telling strokes, and I have yet to see a single smudge of dirtiness in any of his shadows. More astounding still, he does without malice . . . in a territory where malice is both the coin and the curse of the realm.

I cannot remember that any of the ladies, proverbially famous for vanity, took exception to their Skolsky portraits. One, perhaps two, inordinately modest gentlemen did. Why, I can't guess. He did them most merciful justice, and for his kindness was once imprisoned in a slowly descending elevator with a subject so indignant that Mr. Skolsky was momentarily expecting a shove to the bottom of the shaft. Broadway has its battlefields and its war crosses. Columnists must sign their ease and prepare to be first casualties.

But the larger, more constant embarrassment of this gallery of well-knowns must have been, not indignation, but, on the contrary, supplication. No sooner was Mr. Skolsky's series a pronounced success—and it was such a success much sooner than it was a series—than the coy requests began to pour in. He was invited, advised, urged, begged to grow staccato concerning the semi-private lives of almost every semi-private person in New York.

He had me always wondering how he escaped wasting time and space on opaque and uninteresting third-raters. Until I saw that the fun lay all in Skolsky himself, and that he had his own happy way of turning kitchen-maids into Columbines and dullest dogs into blue-ribbon wonders of the Broadway age.

GILBERT W. GABRIEL

CONTENTS

CONTENTS

TIMES SQUARE
TINTYPES

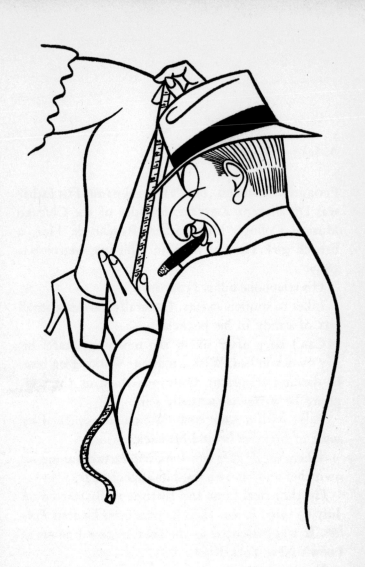

FLORENZ ZIEGFELD. That's his real name. His father was Dr. Florenz Ziegfeld, founder of the Chicago Musical College. His mother, Rosalie de Hez, a French girl. He was born in Chicago, March 21, 1869.

His telephone bill is $50 a day.

Likes to munch sweets. Generally carries a small box of candy in his pocket.

Can't sleep after six in the morning. Starts his day's work in bed. With a masseur working on him, he dictates telegrams. Only one-third of the telegrams he writes are actually sent.

Talks with a nasal tone. Which is mimicked by some of his stars behind his back.

Whenever he goes on a long trip he takes along his own chef and his own food in a special car.

His theatrical fame and fortune really started on July 8, 1907. It was then he produced his first *Follies*. It was presented in the theater now known as Loew's New York Roof.

Knows more ways of escaping process servers than any other man in the world.

He can't keep a secret.

I

Wears lavender-colored shirts, pointed perforated shoes, usually brown, and a hat that costs $40. In the winter he always wears a heavy beaver coat. He hates evening clothes and seldom wears them.

Is an expert tangoist. And in his youth won several prizes for his ballroom dancing.

The one thing in life he can't stand—it drives him nuts—is the sound of drums.

Anna Held was his first wife. He is now married to Billie Burke. The thing he cherishes most is their daughter, Patricia, age thirteen. One day she tried to catch a butterfly and failed. The next day he bought a $500 collection of butterflies for her.

At rehearsals the brim of his hat is turned down. And he wears a brown sweater vest.

Is a wizard with a rifle. Owns about forty guns. Often will stop at a shooting gallery and win a bet from an innocent friend who doesn't know this.

His monument is his theater. He hates to be reminded that the letters "Ziegfeld Theatre" over the marquee are removable.

On his desk there are two gold-plated Continental type telephones. They were made especially for him when he complained that he couldn't hear over the ordinary French phones. The gold is polished daily.

Elephants are his luck charm. Always carries a jade elephant in his vest pocket.

He owns three cars. A Rolls-Royce, a Hispano-

Suiza and a Ford. Has the same license number on all his cars every year.

In his office, on a table in the middle of the room, there is a bronze bust of himself. Next to it is a crystal ball and some elephants of varying sizes. Whenever he is perplexed about something he looks at the statue of himself and rubs the crystal ball with his right hand.

He doesn't know a laugh until someone else laughs.

His pet enemy is Arthur Hammerstein. One day, outside of the New Amsterdam Theatre, a man hit him over the head with an umbrella. To this day he insists that the man mistook him for Arthur Hammerstein.

If his show's a hit he sends the authors gardenias.

His home at Hastings, N. Y., called Burkely Crest, cost nearly a million dollars. The bathroom alone cost $20,000. He has a live bear there and a doll's house (almost large enough to live in) for Patricia. As you enter the estate three parrots greet you by saying: "Hello. Hello. Hello."

Is always pessimistic about new shows. His nickname is "Gloomy Gus."

He uses one perfume, an especially mixed scent called "Parfum Ziegfeld." Uses it to scent his theater just because his nostrils are used to it. He never stopped to think his audience might not like it.

His daughter Patricia gets a percentage of every show he produces.

3

Thrives on publicity. Would rather go to court over a bill and gain the publicity than to pay it immediately. One day he sailed for Europe when an international affair held the front pages. Two days later his press agent received this cable: "Why did you sneak me out of America?"

Loves to go fishing and hunting. His favorite pastime, however, is pitching horseshoes. Every Sunday he sees about seven feature pictures at home in his private theater.

Another of his recreations is yachting. Has a change of apparel for each shift of the wind. Sails gayly down the coast while one of his cars follows along the shore, waiting for him to tire of it.

He has very tender skin on his face. Almost like a baby's. Always gets shaved in his office. He doesn't want men in a public barber shop to see him bleed.

When courting Billie Burke he used to meet her secretly in Grant's Tomb.

If he likes you he is not at all a bad guy.

DAVID BELASCO is America's oldest producer. He was born July 25, 1853, in Howard Street, San Francisco. Eight hours after his mother had arrived from London.

His parents were of Portuguese-Jewish descent. Centuries ago the name was "Valasco."

Claims he feels as spry today as he did at the age of twenty-one. If you doubt it, he'll race up and down the corridor to prove it to you. His one great wish is to die in harness.

He is five feet three. His shoulders droop inward. His eyesight is good, but he rambles a bit when talking. In conversation each succeeding word grows fainter and the last half of his sentences is indistinguishable. Yet the listener understands every word by watching his hands and eyes.

It is his custom to open all his plays on a Tuesday night.

When he is greatly pleased with someone, he quickly digs into his pocket and rewards the party with a nickel or a dime.

Has been at different times in his career a messenger boy, a chore boy in a cigar factory, a clerk in a bookstore, a free-lance reporter, a bareback rider in a circus, a declaimer and a necktie salesman. Somewhere among these various occupations he managed to write his first play. He was only twelve at the time and the opus was called *Jim Black or The Regulator's Revenge*.

The now famous clerical collar can be traced back to his youth, when his idol was Father McGuire. It was hero worship that first led him to imitate the Father in the manner of dress. Later he probably realized that a saint in the theatrical profession would be a novelty.

His collars and ties are made especially for him. Generally wears blue shirts. His shoes are long, pointed, black and buttoned. His hat, a square derby, is also made to order.

He once played Uncle Tom in *Uncle Tom's Cabin*.

Never smokes and seldom drinks. Three sips are enough to make him feel gay.

Actors will work for him cheaper than for any other producer, because they believe he will bring out their hidden talent. He so impresses his feminine office help that they work for him for twenty-five dollars a week in preference to working elsewhere for fifty dollars weekly. At the office they call him "The Governor." He refers to himself as "D. B." His mother's pet name for him was "Wandering Feet."

8

One of his most famous statements is: "Introduce me to a girl and I'm positively bashful. Bring me an actress and I'm her master."

Blanche Bates laid the cornerstone for the present Belasco Theatre, December 5, 1906. It was first called the Stuyvesant Theatre. He renamed it because he wanted a monument.

He enters his office from the stage door. Ascends to it by means of a private elevator. The office is a studio room on the third floor of the Belasco Theatre. There is another entrance on the third floor—an unnoticed door protected by a burglar alarm. Entering this door, you walk through a room filled entirely with glassware. Then comes the Napoleonic Room. Then the Gothic Room. Then a library. Then an indoor garden with a spraying fountain. And then the office proper. His desk is merely a table given to him thirty-three years ago by his mother. It is held together by strings. He also has a sunken Roman bath in the building and spends a great deal of time in it every day.

He is a firm believer in the supernatural. The idea for *The Return of Peter Grimm,* so he states, was given to him in a dream by his mother after her death.

Lives in a hotel in the East Fifties. His home is similar to his office and contains many curios. In one of the clothes closets he has built a miniature cathedral. Many antique clocks decorate the living

9

room. No two of them telling the same time.

He has produced more plays than any other person in the world. Not counting his amateur productions, the figure is three hundred seventy-two. Has never had a penny of outside money in any of his shows. The investment is his own, as are the profits and losses.

Is much interested in electrical effects. In one play, *The Darling of the Gods*, a lighting effect alone occupied the stage for seven minutes. One of his most important contributions to the theater is the hidden footlights.

His favorite color is baby blue. He hates shiny objects. He never has his shoes shined.

When he puts a new play into rehearsal, the first week is spent in the green room of the theater. Here the play is read to the cast by the author or "D. B." personally. Actual rehearsal is never started until the exact settings to be used have been delivered. Every play is rehearsed on the stage of the theater where it is to open.

Rarely sets his plays on paper with his own pen. Two secretaries take care of the mechanical part. He declaims passage after passage, acting out each character in detail, even going through the stage business. It is the duty of one secretary to take down the dialogue. The duty of the other is to record the action. He may work for months, even for years, on one play. Whenever he gets an idea, he makes a note of it and hangs it on the wall in his office. Later these notes are filed and indexed and cross-indexed. When he thinks he has collected enough material, he takes out the notes and starts reciting—that is, writing his new play.

He was once mascot of the local fire department of Vancouver, B. C.

The keynote of his success, he believes, is his great power of concentration. While working on a play his mind is so occupied with it that his secretary has to help him cross the street to protect him.

He carries a brief case on which is inscribed in gold letters: "The Play I am now Writing."

Has in his office a bell which was once the property of George Washington. When he rings, everybody in the building who hears it rushes to him immediately. Rings it on an average of three times a year.

He used to suffer from indigestion. Because whenever he saw anyone eating anything that looked good, without knowing what it was, he would order it. These days he is under a doctor's care and is faithful to his prescribed diet.

When directing Jack Dempsey in *The Big Fight*, he not only instructed Dempsey how to fight but also showed him how to make love to Estelle Taylor.

He was shot at once. The bullet grazed his forehead. The scar is still there. He was trying to protect a woman's honor.

A MAN of note. GEORGE GERSHWIN.

He loves to go shopping. Is always buying presents for friends.

Suffers from indigestion. Every night before retiring he takes agar-agar, a new medicine.

Was born in Brooklyn, September 26, 1898, and came to this country at the age of six weeks. Has two brothers, Ira and Arthur, and one sister, Frances. As a youngster he was the champion roller skater of his neighborhood.

Smokes a cigar out of the side of his mouth and wears a high hat gracefully. He didn't start to smoke until he was twenty.

His father, Morris, because of his unconscious humor, is the life of all the Gershwin parties. Morris has been a designer of fancy uppers for women's shoes, owned several cigar stores, owned a billiard parlor, owned a Turkish bath place and was a bookie. Morris also entertains by imitating a trumpet.

Took his first piano lesson when he was thirteen. At sixteen he was working for Remick's. His boyhood idols were Jerome Kern and Irving Berlin.

The thing he values most is an autographed photograph of King George of England. It bears this inscription: "From George to George."

He wrote his first song when he was fourteen. It was a nameless tango. His second composition (now he had learned to title them) was "Since I Found You." It was never published. His first published song, "When You Want Them You Can't Get Them And When You've Got Them You Don't Want Them," he sold to Harry Von Tilzer for five dollars.

Twice a week he visits an osteopath.

Hates cards. His favorite game is backgammon. Occasionally he shoots craps.

He once worked as relief pianist at Fox's City Theatre. Was fired because an actor complained that he didn't know how to play the piano.

An English publisher sends him copies of rare and first editions of such authors as Galsworthy, Shaw and Barrie in return for an occasional song.

His first piano teacher, whose memory he cherishes, was Charles Hambitzer. His present teacher is Mme. Boulanger in Paris. The first time he went to Paris to study he came back with a trunkful of shirts and ties. On his last trip he returned with a $10,000 organ which he has yet to unpack.

Hard liquor doesn't appeal to him. He likes a glass of real beer. After more than one cocktail his eyes begin to shine.

The first long piece he ever wrote was not "The

Rhapsody in Blue." But one called "135th Street." It was performed by Paul Whiteman in the *Scandals of 1921* for one performance only. It was taken out because it was too sad.

He is very particular about his clothes which are made to order. Even when he made only $25 a week he spent $22 for a pair of shoes.

Writes whenever the mood seizes him. He may have just returned home after a party and still attired in his evening clothes he will sit down at the piano. Or he may compose wearing pajamas, or a bathrobe—or even nude.

He is physically very strong. Especially his arms which are powerful. He is a swell wrestler.

His brother Ira writes the lyrics for his songs. Before, Irving Caesar and Buddy De Sylva had the honor.

"The Rhapsody in Blue" was played for the first time, February 12, 1924, at Aeolian Hall. It took him three months to write it. It took him eight months to write, "An American in Paris." His first real popular song hit was "Swanee." This was written for the revue that opened the Capitol Theatre.

Is bashful about playing the piano at parties. He has to be coaxed. Once he starts, however, you can't stop him. He says: "You see the trouble is, when I don't play I don't have a good time."

In the volume called *Great Composers As Children* he is the only living composer listed.

One evening the family was discussing the new Einstein paper. George expressed his surprise at the compactness of the scientific vocabulary. He said: "Imagine working for twenty years and putting your results into three pages?" "Well," said Papa Gershwin, "it was probably very small print."

Whenever his sister Frances has an audition for a job he goes along and plays the piano for her.

His two favorite eating places are Dinty Moore's and his mother's. At Moore's he generally orders vegetable soup, double lamb chops and rice pudding. At his mother's he is fond of cold bortsch.

He is always saying: "I don't do enough work."

When rehearsing a new show he spends hours singing his songs to the chorus.

Victor Herbert once offered to teach him orchestration but died. He studied at Columbia for two months. Then quit. Everything he knows about this he taught himself.

When in Vienna last year a party was given for him. The chef was ordered to make blue ice cream in honor of the "Rhapsody." This couldn't be done so the ice cream was served with American flags.

He has a bit of the Puritan in him. If he sees his sister sitting with her dress above her knees, he pulls it down.

He has a secret passion to be an actor.

HE wanted a monument, so he built the Roxy Theatre and called it, with his usual simplicity, "The Cathedral of the Motion Picture."

It is a living tribute to a great man. It oozes his personality. It is so great that it has even absorbed the man. He lives in his monument. Has an apartment adjacent to his business office on the sixth floor. The man—oh, yes, Samuel Lionel Rothafel. Everybody calls him what he calls his theater, ROXY.

He averages eighteen hours a day in the theater. When asked to make a speech on, "What I Do With My Leisure Time," he was obliged to change the subject.

His favorite food is hamburger steak chopped very fine with onions. His favorite delicacy is hot dogs.

He has clothes in four places. At the theater, at home and at two golf clubs. Recently it took two men four weeks to make a complete inventory of his clothing.

In the motion picture industry his position is unique. He is the leader of presentations, the originator of the atmospheric prologue. Also institutional movie houses, introducing staff uniforms and military ushers.

Has a habit of putting a final touch to a discussion by saying, "Applesauce. Bunk. Boloney."

The first movie house he ever owned seated two hundred fifty people. The chairs were removable. Every time there was a big funeral there wasn't any show. They needed the chairs.

Calls everybody by their first name or not at all.

His mascot is a black cat called "Lindy." The cat walked in from the street the day Lindbergh hopped off for Paris. It has been there ever since.

He speaks with a lisp. Always has a sob in his throat. It's a great radio voice. "Hello, everybody!"

His favorite eating place is a lunch wagon.

Every Thursday he spends the entire night rehearsing next week's show. During rehearsals he is a fiery dynamo. Exhorting. Scolding. Unreasonable. Demanding the impossible and getting it. He always refers to the actors and stage crew as "My Children."

In his apartment at the Roxy he has a valet, a chef and a butler.

His ushers are put through drills by a "Devil Dog" every morning.

His favorite exercise is handball. Is very proud of the fact that he plays well enough to beat Benny Leonard.

The orchestra pit is so large that Arthur Hopkins

once remarked to him: "Don't let the Shuberts see it or they'll want to build a theater there."

Every Friday at one o'clock he sits in the last row of the balcony and watches the first performance of the show he has rehearsed all night. Under his chair is coiled an elaborate affair which enables him to broadcast directions backstage. He speaks through a mouthpiece. The audience is unable to hear a word. But the players onstage, the electricians, the property room, the music library and the projection booth receive instructions.

After this he retires to his apartment to get some sleep. He is up again at four watching the second performance. To see that all his corrections have been made.

After this he plays two-handed casino. He plays poker with his staff and loses continuously. He complains they "play too close to the vest."

His father and sister use to operate a movie house in Forrest City, Pennsylvania.

Really believes he bears a striking resemblance to Napoleon both in character and in appearance.

He has four secretaries. Yet does most of the work himself, for he believes he is the only person who can do the things that made Roxy Roxy.

His business correspondence starts "My dear little girl." It ends with, "Yours truly, S. L. Rothafel."

Is a great golf fiend. When he has nothing to do

in the office he shoots a paper golf ball around.

Was once a marine, a baseball player and a bartender.

Upon learning that Hugo Riesenfeld attended the University of Paris, he said to him: "From now on, Hugo, you're going to be known as Dr. Riesenfeld."

Has a great respect for people who speak English correctly.

His idea of a good joke is to sit a visitor under the mantelpiece in his office and wait for that party to bump his head when rising.

He cannot read a note of music nor can he play an instrument. However, he has a wonderful memory. He can whistle the entire score of *Pinafore*. While he is conducting the orchestra some of the musicians will not look at the baton for fear they will make a mistake.

"GIVE THIS LITTLE GIRL A GREAT BIG HANDCUFF"

GIVE this little girl a big hand. TEXAS GUINAN.

Never eats meats, but must have at least a dozen oranges a day.

She was raised in a convent. Loretta Convent, Waco, Tex. Was the same old kid even in those days. She would climb to the top of the church steeple and take the dinger out of the bell. Her real name is Mary Louise Guinan.

Once was in motion pictures. Made Westerns and was known as the "Female William S. Hart."

Her home in New York is on Eighth Street. Just on the northern edge of Greenwich Village. Claims she wouldn't live anywhere else in this town of ours.

She possesses the quickest feminine wit on Broadway.

Lives alone. Her mother lives several doors away. Spends most of the time at her daughter's place.

Her house looks like an antique shop. Pictures. Bric-a-brac. Mirrors. Odd furniture. Cushions. Gilded draperies. They all clutter the place. Chinese incense burns continuously.

There are nineteen floor lamps in the living room.

Recently she abandoned the expression, "Hello, sucker!" Customers began to take it seriously.

When she finishes at the club she goes horseback riding in Central Park or visiting. It is nothing for her to drop in on friends at seven in the morning and sit on their beds talking until noon.

She likes noise, rhinestone heels, customers, plenty of attention and red velvet bathing suits.

The hardest thing in the world she finds is sleeping. Always takes an aspirin tablet to quiet her nerves before retiring.

When not certain of a man's name she calls him Fred.

Has a parrot who can say only two things. One is "telephone." The other is "go to hell."

At home she never drinks coffee. At the club black coffee is her favorite drink.

She never touches liquor.

Is very proud of her press clippings and keeps a scrapbook. So religiously does she keep this book that reference to the "Texas Chain Gang," an article by Ernest Booth which appeared in the *American Mercury*, is clipped as personal publicity.

She takes three puffs of a cigarette and it is gone.

She once lost thirty-five pounds in two weeks by taking pepper and mustard baths.

In an interview she once stated that she wants her funeral to be the speediest ever given. A cop on a motorcycle is to lead it.

Since, she has made more plans. Jazz syncopators are to render torrid tunes. College songs are to be sung boisterously as the coffin is lowered into the grave. The wake is to be held at her night club.

In her bedroom there is only one window. It is covered by four curtains to keep the sunlight out.

She is very fond of jewelry. The bigger it is the better she likes it. She wears jewelry on her bosom, fingers, wrists, arms, ears and occasionally the heels of her slippers.

She frequently wears red stockings.

Was shot once. By herself. It was a stage accident while she was on the road in *The Gay Musician*. She was rushed to a hospital in a locomotive engine. She had a steel tube in her side for over a year. Today all that remains of that incident is a slight blemish, the only mark on her body.

She is only comfortable when sitting on two chairs.

She has six uncles. They are all Catholic priests.

Recently it was stated that she sleeps on her left side and likes carrots. To which Mme. Guinan retorted:

"I wonder how that guy knew I liked carrots."

She sleeps on her right side in a long silk gay colored nightgown and likes strawberries.

She makes funny noises with her teeth when she laughs.

Her luck charm is a padlock.

27

A HOODLUM was picked up on the streets of Toronto for raiding fruit stands. A stern judge saw that the law took care of him and said: "You're a bad egg. No good will come from you." The bad egg was GEORGE WHITE.

He has 140 neckties. They are all black.

Weighs 140 pounds. Has never been known to eat fast or walk slowly.

His father was a Jewish garment manufacturer on Delancey Street. There were ten other children in the family. He stole fruit, blacked boots, danced, sold flowers and papers. As a kid he had no great ambition.

Delights in playing practical jokes on his stars. Almost to the point of ruining their performance in his own show.

He has a patent-leather hair comb. Pays great attention to his hair. Always carries a bottle of petroleum oil which he alternates between rubbing on his hair and drinking.

His début as a dancer was made in "Piggy" Donovan's saloon on the Bowery. He was then "Swifty," the messenger boy. Was delivering telegrams when he asked the piano player to let him hoof. He collected $12.30 which was tossed at him. He threw away the remainder of the telegrams. Two were marked: "DEATH—RUSH."

Is thirty-eight years old. The first thing he notices about a woman is her legs. Then her form. After that her face. Is on the credit side of the matrimonial ledger and never expects to get married.

He has a Jap butler, Shei, who gets tight on his best Scotch. He won't fire him. He likes his cooking.

Once was kicked out of a saloon by a singing waiter named Irving Berlin.

Was a stable boy and a jockey. He followed the horses around the country. Later, his love for the races cost him $850,000 in eighteen months. Once dropped $100,000 on one race. Then he swore off. Hasn't been at a race track for the past five years.

He was the first vaudeville performer to do a dance on skiis.

Generally gets to bed at about four in the morning and is up at twelve. Spends a part of each day playing with the mechanical toys he brings back from his yearly trips to Paris.

His hobby is selling tickets in the box office. Some day he hopes to be able to tell Ziegfeld there is "Standing Room Only."

Does things on the spur of the moment. Five minutes before he sailed for Paris a year ago he purchased a Park Avenue apartment house. Merely because he liked one apartment in the building. He lives in an apartment on Seventh Avenue because he doesn't want to pay the Park Avenue rent he charges.

His middle name is Alviel which he uses only on checks.

Among his major hates are first nights, paper napkins, barbers with a selling complex and crowds —except at his own shows.

He owns a Rolls-Royce which can be seen standing outside of his theater. He generally walks home between the car tracks in Times Square. He won the auto on a bet. On first hearing "The Birth of the Blues," he bet a music publisher a Rolls-Royce it would be a song hit. It was.

Produced and operated six annual editions of his *Scandals*, each doing an approximate gross business of $1,250,000 without an office. In those days his office was in his pocket.

In selecting chorus girls he generally allows Lew Brown to help him do the picking.

He hasn't read a book for as long as he can remember. He never attends a performance of a dramatic play. He sees all the musicals.

Cried only once in his life. That was when he read Burns Mantle's criticism of his first show which said: "The Scandals of 1919 prove that a hoofer should stick to his dancing."

His sole exercise is a walk around the Reservoir in Central Park. On these occasions he takes along a male companion or a thin walking stick.

Always wears blue serge suits, black shoes, white silk shirts and black ties. One day he wore a gray suit and the stage doorman, failing to recognize him, wouldn't let him in.

His favorite meal is one consisting of caviar and champagne. He can eat a pound of caviar at a sitting. Is a very slow eater. It takes him an hour to consume a sandwich.

Not so long ago a woman, Rose Janousek, sent him a package containing a revolver and fifty rounds of ammunition merely because she admired him.

On Sunday nights he generally takes his best girl to the Roxy. While looking at the picture they hold hands.

When his ego rises, he modestly enough calls Broadway—The Great White Way—believing it was named after him.

SAMUEL SHIPMAN. When he was graduated from Columbia this line appeared under his picture in the college book: "God Makes Some Strange Things."

His first play, which he wrote at the age of twelve, was something called *Justice*. It was performed at the Jewish Educational Alliance.

He is marvelously unkempt. Even after he has had a shave and a haircut he needs a shave and a haircut.

As a kid he wore phony jewelry to appear rich.

Writes all his plays in Atlantic City. He engages a suite in one of the exclusive hotels. He always takes two stenographers and a collaborator with him. He dictates everything he writes. Paces the floor and is often in another room shouting the lines. The stenographers work in relays, one resting while the other is taking the dictation.

He never sleeps more than four hours a day. And always one of these hours is between five and six in the morning.

He made a million dollars in royalties from *Friendly Enemies* and *East Is West*. So did Wall Street.

Likes to drink and play with tea. Is always pouring

the tea from the glass to the saucer and then back into the glass.

Has only one superstition. That is he must start and finish his plays on a Tuesday. It doesn't matter if the Tuesdays are months apart.

He once taught English in an East Side school.

Everything he does he describes as "terrific."

Has only one superstition; that is, theatrical notables. Eugene O'Neill, for example, he believes is only an intellectualized Theodore Kramer. Claims the only thing he likes about George Jean Nathan is H. L. Mencken. A. H. Woods is his favorite producer. Because whenever he hands that impresario a flop Woods never cries, but merely says: "It's all right, sweetheart; try again."

He rarely eats meat. His favorite meal is one composed solely of caviar.

Likes to go prowling about the city at night and often sets out at midnight, alone.

The sight of fish fascinates him. He is a frequent visitor at the Aquarium.

He never hangs up anything. His clothes are sprawled about the house. On entering he tosses his hat anywhere. His coat is dropped on the living room floor; the vest on the bedroom floor. His trousers he carefully places at the foot of his bed. He dresses faster than a fireman.

To date he has had twelve collaborators. His favorite is John B. Hymer because Hymer understands him.

He wants to know everything before anyone else.

Never reads a book during the winter. Every summer he goes for a vacation in the Catskill Mountains, taking two valises full of books with him.

Doesn't like young girls. Never goes out with a lady under thirty-five.

Never falls in love with an actress. His sweetheart is a nonprofessional. Her parents, however, dislike everything connected with the theater and won't allow him in the house.

His ambition in life is to write the libretto of an opera and have it presented at the Metropolitan Opera House.

He suffers from indigestion. His secretary carries his pills and reminds him when he has indigestion.

At Columbia he studied playwriting under Brander Matthews, who gave him a C minus. He asked that his mark be raised and Matthews asked why. Shipman then pulled out a contract for a play he had just sold. Matthews merely replied: "It's the old story. Theory is theory and practice is practice."

He covered the Ruth Snyder case for a tabloid newspaper.

Never cleans his shoes on the outside but only inside. This, he claims, is healthy for the feet.

He can recite most of Ibsen's plays from memory.

While writing a play his teeth become loose; in fact, so loose that he can pluck them. To date he has plucked six. The minute the play is finished his teeth tighten. He is continually visiting dentists because of this condition.

The greatest disappointment one can get in life, he believes, is meeting somebody one has heard a lot about.

One evening at the Lambs Club Eugene O'Neill was playing poker with a group of playwrights. After losing all his money O'Neill offered to play on his ability as a dramatist. After another hour of heavy losing O'Neill got up and started for home. As he was leaving the doorman said: "Good night, Mr. Shipman."

The only time he ever combs his hair is before going to bed.

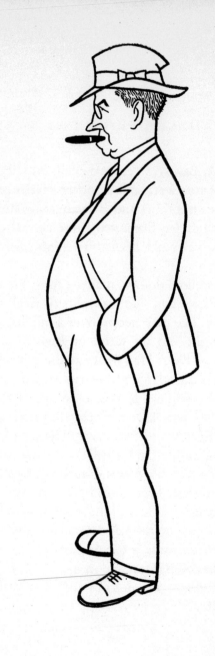

"THE GAMBLER FROM THE WEST"

WILLIAM A. BRADY. Everybody calls him "Pop."

He owns five watches but never carries one. Always guesses the time, and is fairly accurate.

Was born in San Francisco, June 19, 1863. Until he was five years old he had a Chinese lady for a nursemaid.

Lost a million dollars many times. He owned *Within the Law* and sold his rights to Arch Selwyn for $10,000. The play netted over a million. Jeanne Eagels brought him the script of *Rain* to produce. He said: "I no like." Had *Broadway* in rehearsal and shelved it on the advice of George M. Cohan. That was another million. He was to be one of the promoters of the Carpentier-Dempsey fight. Had words with Jack Kearns and withdrew. The gate for that battle was a million and a half.

Last year while in a hospital nursing a broken leg, his doctors allowed him to read plays instead of taking sleeping tablets. He read the much rejected *Street Scene*. He is now on his way to another million.

That A in his name is for Augustus.

Always has been interested in sports. He managed James J. Corbett, Jim Jeffries and Youssouf, "the terrible Turk."

He wears a large brown felt hat. Always has a cigar in his mouth. Even when sleeping. Once was discovered in bed in a mass of flames which a friend put out with a fire extinguisher.

His idea of a good time is to buy champagne for the house. His favorite drink is a tall glass of rye. During the Corbett-Sullivan fight he consumed two quarts of whiskey.

Never carries a cane. Except when looking for a fight.

Alice Brady is his daughter by his first wife, Rose Marie Rene. William Brady, Jr., is his son by his present wife, Grace George.

Hasn't an automobile although he did own one for twenty years. His doctor ordered him to give it up because he never took a walk. He seldom crosses the street alone. Always waits for the red light.

He once cut cards with Arnold Rothstein. One cut for $45,000 and won.

Is sad because he isn't allowed to attend prize fights. He takes and gives every blow himself. The last fight he saw was the Dempsey-Sharkey encounter. After it was over he was so exhausted that he had to be carried three blocks to a taxi.

Loves music. His favorites are "Faust," "Killarney," "Massa's In The Cold, Cold Ground" and "Believe Me If All Those Endearing Young Charms."

He likes to act and resents being called a ham. His most recent performance was in *A Free Soul*. Jumped into the leading rôle on only an hour's notice. Placed the script on a table in the scene. Whenever he forgot a line he walked to the table.

When a young man he was a natty dresser. Today clothes don't interest him. Used to wear many diamonds. Recently gave them all to Grace George for a necklace.

Reads all newspapers, trashy magazines and the highbrow ones. His favorite reading matter is the Congressional Record. Reads every line of it during sessions of Congress. Senator Heflin is his favorite comic.

Cleveland, Harrison, McKinley, Roosevelt, Taft, Wilson, Harding, Coolidge and Hoover are the Presidents he knew and knows personally.

His choice of food depends upon what he is drinking. Has a cast-iron stomach. Is especially fond of Mexican tamales.

He claims the toughest job he ever had was managing Louis Mann for five years.

With Sir August Hannis he sneaked into Windsor Castle and disguised as a chorus man appeared before the King and Queen of England in a command performance of *The Bohemian Girl*.

Once desired to be the youngest man to climb Pike's Peak. Halfway up he changed his mind and took the train back.

Can recite offhand any speech that Shakespeare ever wrote. Loves to see Shakespearean plays, but not to produce them.

Was arrested and put in prison once. That, when he broke up a street meeting of Dowie, the Evangelist, who was lecturing in front of the old Madison Square Garden.

He started wearing glasses at forty. He was told to do so when he was twenty.

Lives in a penthouse atop a fifteen-story building he owns in Fifty-fifth Street. Spends his evenings there listening to the radio and looking out over Broadway. Wants the last thing he looks at before he dies to be a flash of the White Lights.

His credo is, "The Lord is always good to honest gamblers."

EARL CARROLL. He has a throne, a palace and a title. His throne is an antique Chinese chair. His palace is the theater bearing his name. His title is "The Earl of Seventh Avenue."

He is extremely polite to everyone. Expects people to be that way to him. Nobody can really get close to him.

He suffers from insomnia.

Was born in Pittsburgh, September 16, 1892. Has two brothers, Norman and James, and one sister, Alice. The brothers don't look like him or each other. The sister could pass for his twin. When a small boy he was dressed in a white sailor suit.

If he sees a pretty girl on the street he will stop her and ask her if she wants to go on the stage.

At the age of sixteen he stood in the center of Nanking Road, China, with only forty-five cents in his pocket.

His office is backstage of his theater. A rug, the color of pigeon blood, covers the floor. His desk is enclosed in a wall. The pressing of a button shoots it forward. He uses a sword for a paperweight. Has a statue of Buddha here. And a refrigerator with

Chinese letters written on it. The letters spell—happiness. In the rear of the office there is a secret panel through which he can make a hasty exit.

He can't wear a shirt with a collar attached. And all of his vests must be double-breasted.

Once wrote a song with Enrico Caruso. It was "Dreams Of Long Ago." Immediately after joining the army he wrote a song called: "When I'm Through With the Arms of the Army I'll Come Back to the Arms of You."

Always throws a party for himself on his birthday.

His favorite type of beauty for the stage is a tall blonde. His own personal taste, however, runs to slender brunettes.

During the war he was a lieutenant in the United States Air Service. He was the first man to land an airplane in Central Park.

While rehearsing a new show he wears a sand-colored smock. His shirt is minus collar and tie. He stands in the orchestra. Has a telephone operator's apparatus on his head. Through this he gives instructions backstage, under the stage and in the electrician's booth plastered on the back wall of the balcony. To his left is a small table. His secretary, Miss Ruth, sits here and takes memos. During all this he is continually drinking Poland mineral water and chewing gum.

Likes to use perfume. His two favorites are Caron's Acaciosa and Gabilla's Jasmin. He sprays his throat with perfume daily.

On April 10, he and his two brothers and sister always journey to Pittsburgh to visit their mother's grave. On Mother's Day he sends flowers.

Was the first man in New York to own a "Starlight Bungalow," now known as a penthouse. His was located on the roof of 729 Seventh Avenue. He called it "Top o' the World." He likes to live high and now resides on the top floor of a tall apartment hotel.

The expressions he uses most frequently are: "No dice." "You take the bump." "Must I do everything myself."

Always looks as if he needs a haircut from the back. But never from the front. He is very careful about his hair. Every night he has a woman massage his scalp.

He never interviews a chorus girl without a third person in the room.

Carries all his keys in his hip pocket attached to a penknife and pencil set. From the chain hangs a charm. When you spin the charm it says, "I Love You."

Is always complaining that his feet are cold.

His best friend is W. R. Edrington, who built the Carroll Theatre for him. In his office there hangs a frame, containing two photographs. One is of George Washington. The other of Mr. Edrington. Under

Washington's picture is the caption: "The Father of Our Country. Born February 22, 1732." Under Edrington's picture is the caption: "The Father of Our Theatre. Born February 22, 1872."

He presented the most expensive show ever produced—and also the cheapest one. *Fioretta* cost in the neighborhood of $325,000. *White Cargo* cost him exactly $68.

The only things he has made to order are his pajamas and handkerchiefs. The handkerchiefs are made and initialed in Paris. The pajamas are double-breasted and designed by himself.

His motto is: "I would rather you were less talented than less loyal." Until recently he had this hanging on a wall with a picture of Peggy Joyce under it.

Has a private phone in his office. But can never call from the outside because he can't remember the number. The phone is an especially designed one—it was made by his electrician. There isn't another like it in the country. It sings a song while you're waiting for your number.

He's a big baby when he's sick.

His great ambition in life is to be instrumental in changing the parole law in the United States prisons.

FANNIE BRICE. She was born at the stroke of midnight on October 29, 1892. Her square monicker is Fannie Borach.

She enjoys a good cry.

Hasn't a long list of friends. But those she has she can tap for anything.

She took the tag of Brice from John Brice, a next-door neighbor. He is now a watchman on the Ninth Avenue elevated. She told him that some day he'd see his name in lights.

Is a good judge of diamonds, furs and the value of real estate.

There is one thing in this world she can't stand. That is cream in her coffee. It makes her sick.

She is the proud mother of two children. A girl of nine and a boy of seven. Has one brother, Lew, in the theatrical business. Also has one sister, Caroline, who believes that she would be a great actress if she didn't suffer from asthma.

Her hobby is taking photographs of bedrooms. She has a picture of every bedroom she ever lived in.

Made her stage début at Keeney's Theater in Brooklyn on amateur night. She won first prize singing, "When You're Not Forgotten by the Girl You Can't Forget."

The only instrument she can play is the piano. That is, if hunting for notes with two fingers can be called playing.

Her father owned a string of saloons. He was known as "French Charlie." Her mother really ran the saloons, for "French Charlie" was always playing pinochle.

When traveling she takes an electric stove with her. She'll cook for anybody who wants to eat.

She once worked in a movie house on Eighty-third Street and Third Avenue. Here she sang songs, sold tickets and painted signs. Her salary was $8 a week.

The biggest surprises she ever got, good or bad, were from herself.

Is one of the best dressed women in the theater. Has her dresses designed especially for her by Kiviette. While in Hollywood she made dresses for Dolores Costello and Norma Talmadge. She has thirty dresses she hasn't gotten to yet.

The moon makes her serious.

When watching Fannie perform her mother always says to the people sitting about her: "That's my daughter. She's good, isn't she?"

She dislikes people who are perfect and have everything. Believes that such people miss something in life.

After she sang "My Man" for the first time her salary was raised from $1,000 to $3,000 weekly.

Her present husband is Billy Rose, who also writes her songs for her. Her nickname for him is "Putsy."

She'd walk ten miles if she could window shop on the way. Otherwise she wouldn't walk two blocks.

Her first comedy song was "Sadie Salome." She sang it merely to help Irving Berlin, then a newcomer, along. It started her on the road to fame and fortune.

She is a card shark.

When it is her turn to name the greatest actor in the world she cheers long and loud for Muni Weisenfrend.

Is never nervous on an opening night. Ten minutes before the opening curtain of *Fioretta* she was busy selling hats to chorus girls.

When signing checks she spells it "Fanny." In the bright lights of Broadway she insists that it be "Fannie."

She was once a soubrette in a Hurtig and Seamon burlesque show.

Whenever she visits her mother she hears these two things: "Oh, did I cook a good soup yesterday. It was like gold." And—"Fannie, save your money."

She never dresses in the morning until after the bed has been made.

As a kid her ambition was to work in a candy

store. So she could eat all the candy she wanted. To-day her ambition is to write songs because Jolson does.

Likes to play the horses. Once was given a false tip and bet $400 on a horse that had never won a race. Through a fluke the horse managed to totter over the line a winner. That night the bookmaker not only delivered the money to her but also the horse.

As far as a favorite dish goes she is torn between an acquired taste for fried pork chops and a natural love for kippered herring.

No matter how hard she may try, she can't say cinema, panorama and aluminum.

She summed up the Hollywood situation better than anyone else when she said: "I was out there eight months. I worked five weeks and got three years' pay."

At her wedding to Billy Rose she had a man, Jay Brennan, serve as bridesmaid.

Claims she never feels better than when she is expecting a baby.

THE American Gorki. He found that hoboing was the road to success. JIM TULLY.

The first thing one notices about him is his flaming red hair. He is five feet three and weighs 163 pounds. His skin is sun drunk. His hands are small and pudgy. He has the thighs of a burlesque queen. Standing, his body like a question mark, he appears ready to leap.

He works and talks at a breakneck pace.

He bites his finger nails.

His mother died when he was four. His father was a ditch digger. His uncle a horse thief. He was in an orphanage until eleven years old. Here, for his ability to memorize the preacher's sermon and say catechism he won a rosary. But a more pious kid stole it.

Wears only five-dollar neckties and has his suits made to order by an anarchist tailor in Hollywood.

Is very proud that Mencken and Nathan are his pals and drink beer with him. Is prouder of this than their esteem for his books.

Started his literary career by writing fake stories for a "True Confession" magazine. One of his prize yarns was *The Memoirs of a Japanese Geisha Girl*.

His philosophy of life is: "What the hell—the grave ends everything."

As a youth he looked forward to becoming the world's greatest bank robber. Gave up the idea when told by a railroad detective he would be caught easily. Because no other person on earth could possibly look like him.

His first book, *Beggars of Life,* he submitted to four publishers simultaneously. The four accepted.

Likes to write in the first person. Believes a direct lie is always more convincing.

Was once a prize fighter. His pugilistic career ended in a California ring when he was knocked out in the first round and remained unconscious for twenty-four hours.

Combs his hair once a day whether it needs it or not.

The only thing he fears is a smart-aleck interviewer.

He has slept on a park bench, in H. L. Mencken's bed, under a freight train, at the Algonquin, and on cold, barren ground, his closed eyes staring at the stars. No matter where he sleeps, he snores.

His name when a hobo was Cincy Red.

Always finds out where people were born, their age, likes and dislikes, and secret sorrows by the second meeting.

He would like to conduct a society column for a newspaper.

Never wore a dress suit in his life. Thinks he would look like a chorus boy if he did.

His father, 78 years old, is still alive. He sends his dad press clippings, good and bad, periodically. His father is a bit disappointed because Jim didn't become a champion prize fighter.

James Branch Cabell is his favorite American author.

He is very moody. Has intense fits of melancholy and terrible laughter.

Doesn't think he should be judged by what he says about his former friends in interviews but by the way he writes.

When interviewing he never takes notes. A week later he writes the interview from impressions.

He easily recognizes his own ability and is annoyed by those who don't.

He wears high-laced tan shoes. They are made to order for him and imported from London.

From force of habit he greets an old friend with: "Did you eat yet?"

He lives and works in Hollywood. Writes in a big, oblong room on the second floor of his house. The room is lined with books from floor to ceiling. Has a flat, square desk with a swivel chair. A beer barrel is within swinging distance. He calls his house "One More Illusion."

In writing a book he does not strive for literary

style. Claims he writes naturally. Just as if he were writing a letter to a harlot.

He doesn't smoke.

Jarnegan is his favorite character in all history. Claims that whenever he feels lonely and depressed he sits down and talks things over with him.

Makes women think his novels belie him because of his soft speech with them. When with men, however, he is just like his novels—turbulent and violent and cussing.

The two greatest guys in the world as far as he is concerned, are George Jean Nathan and Oklahoma Red.

He has a yen for beautiful and beautifully dressed women.

He dreads the thought that some day he won't be alive.

BY GEORGE M. COHAN

HE's a dancer and a singer and a song writer and a master of slang and an actor and a director and a producer and a playwright and a philanthropist and he's GEORGE M. COHAN.

The "M" stands for Michael. Hates to be called George by anyone he thinks is not entitled to use it.

Comes from a family of hoofers. Later famous as "The Four Cohans." He was always on the stage. When only a baby his parents parked him backstage in a basket while they did their act.

He is very charitable. Never gives to societies, but takes care of individual cases. This is one subject he will not speak about. Yet without exaggeration he has given away over a million dollars.

At rehearsals he is in the aisles, on the stage and once was discovered halfway up the proscenium.

His finances are in the hands of Dennis O'Brien. Never knew how much money he had and doesn't today. If left to himself he would write his fortune away. He is one of the wealthiest men in the show business.

His shoes cost $45 a pair. They are handmade. Orders half a dozen pairs at a time.

He sent George Fuller Golden to Colorado for his health. Did this unsolicited and handed Golden $10,000 in cash. Told him to write for more when that was gone. This is merely one of thousands of cases.

Gave his mother the entire royalties of *Get Rich Quick Wallingford* as a Christmas present.

First man to use the American flag to "stop the show." Also the first to glorify it on the stage. He has been called the "Yankee Doodle Boy." Is also said to be a representative American type. Of all things, he was born on July 4. The year, 1878.

Nothing that he ever wrote had an unclean line or situation.

He hasn't temperament. Doesn't wear the high hat. Just the same old felt or derby tilted on the side.

Prefers the company of theatrical folks.

He writes all his stuff with a yellow pencil on yellow paper.

He is the only man who ever turned out musical comedies single-handed. Beginning with *Little Johnny Jones*, he has written the music and lyrics, the book, staged the dances, rehearsed the cast and orchestra, arranged settings and costumes, and played in them.

Wrote over one hundred plays and signed only forty.

A great deal of his charity, in addition to money, has been in the form of song numbers and acts. Gave

66

these away to help struggling performers. He didn't receive any payment nor credit lines. A popular pastime was sending him manuscripts to be "Cohanized."

After watching a show at a dress rehearsal, he knows exactly how much of it will click. Has never gone wrong on one of these predictions. No man in the world understands the audience as well as he.

He rejected the play *Broadway* and advised William A. Brady not to produce it.

Was the first actor to own an automobile. He paid $2,000 for it. People said only an actor would do a thing like that.

He does not mourn for "the good old days." After over twenty years on Broadway he can still compete with the new blood. He considers Broadway of to-day merely a mess of lights.

Cannot and will not write a part for a Jewish character. He claims he doesn't understand them.

Is a baseball and prize-fight fan. He is very clever with his fists.

Once he was playing baseball and objected to the presence of a colored chap because the fellow got on his nerves. He tolerated him for two innings. He then picked up a bat and chased him out of the park, down two blocks. All of the players were anxious about Cohan's safety. When he got back they told him the fellow he chased was Joe Walcott, the prize fighter.

67

Was the first man to collect royalties for vaudeville skits.

Isn't particular about his clothes. But is fussy about his haircuts. Often has his Astor Hotel barber cut it three times before he is satisfied.

He has written over a thousand songs. He thinks of the music and lyrics of a new song at the same time. The bugle called and he wrote "Over There" in five minutes. The original copy of "Over There" is now in the Harvard Museum among rare and precious American manuscripts.

Of all the songs he has written he considers "Venus—My Shining Star" the best. Of all his plays his favorite is *The Tavern*.

Likes to experiment with human beings. His hobby is watching them act out of their environment. Once took all the waiters and bus boys of the Savoy Hotel, London, and treated them to a night of night life. The next morning there wasn't any service in the hotel. He is still famous there.

Considers *Arizona* the best play he ever saw, but he won't go to see the musical version of it.

Is responsible for Douglas Fairbanks breaking into the movies.

One of his favorite pastimes is riding in the subway looking at people.

The biggest laugh he ever got was when a ham comic told him to save his money.

His play, *Forty-five Minutes from Broadway*,

started a real estate boom in New Rochelle and put that place on the map. Today it's a big city only thirty minutes from Broadway.

He takes three baths a day.

His favorite story is about the angel who said he had a show in Buffalo which cost $15,000 and then asked: "Is that good?" He likes to tell about E. F. Albee "shilling" trade in rainy days into Keith's Bijou in Boston with the words: "It's a dollar for an umbrella; go inside and stay dry for a dime."

His first press notice of recognition was in the Buffalo *Advertiser*. He wrote it himself.

Never writes a show completely. He writes the first act and puts it into rehearsal. While it's in rehearsal he writes the second. Puts that in rehearsal and then writes the third.

He detests imitations of himself.

He once did a sister act in vaudeville.

As he looks back at the now famous Equity strike he believes it would make a swell book for a musical comedy.

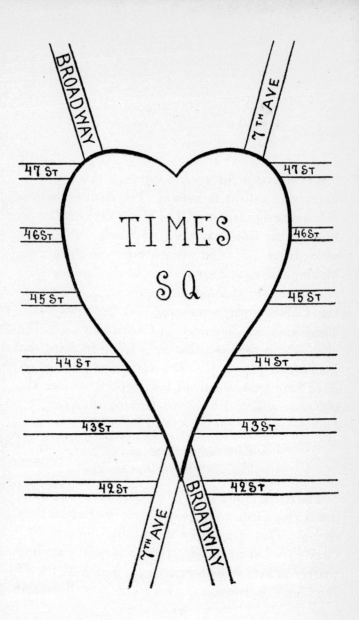

MY STREET

FORTY-SECOND Street and Seventh Avenue . . .
Everybody calls it Broadway. The Rialto Theatre.
A hanging sign says it is "The House Of Hits". . . .
But the big line is at the Paramount . . . Sight-
seeing buses . . . Old women sitting in them . . .
Making a living as decoys . . . See the Bowery . . .
A lecture tour through Chinatown . . . Why, all
the Chinks own restaurants on Broadway . . .
There ain't no Chinamen in Chinatown . . . The
chap who is shouting that he is going to point out
the historic places . . . Did you know he only ar-
rived here from Portland last week? . . . See the
old man selling *The Birth Control Review* . . .
He's doing it for the wife and kiddies. . . .

> *"A million horns from motor cars,*
> *A million lights that dim the stars . . ."*

The Astor Hotel . . . Must have been nice when
it was a big farm . . . More people live outside than
in . . . That drug store diagonally opposite . . .
Gray's . . . You know, there's where you buy
theater tickets at half-price . . . Best seats for all
the "hits" in town . . . Isn't that a well-dressed

man? . . . Tuxedo . . . High hat . . . He's got
class . . . Sure has poise . . . Must be some big
society fellow . . . Wait a moment and his shirt
will light up, advertising a brand of cigar . . .

> *"That's Broadway, Broadway*
> *Heart of the World . . ."*

Loew's New York Roof . . . It's called the old
men's club . . . They go there to sleep . . . Did
you know it once had an elegant French name and
housed the first Ziegfeld *Follies?* . . . There's a nut
embarrassing couples by trying to make the girl take
a rose and make the fellow pay for it . . . Another
Nedick thirst station . . . Hungry, have a hot dog,
too . . . Just like Coney Island . . . A shabby,
fate-beaten old man . . . Once was a great archi-
tect and built many theaters . . . He now haunts
the lobbies of those theaters . . .

> *"A painted smile, a hard-luck tale,*
> *A helping hand—they're all for sale,*
> *On Broadway, Broadway. . . ."*

A Lucky Strike display station . . . Try to edge
your way near the window . . . The blonde is
worth seeing . . . Better than most chorus girls
. . . Don't have to pay $5.50 either . . . The fight
at Madison Square Garden round for round in the
doorway of a sheet music shop . . . And if you're
interested in art, you can look at the picture postal

cards also . . . Childs . . . See them tossing buckwheat cakes . . . This is their Broadway place . . .
Only the best performers work here . . . No newcomers . . . The crowd is too large and critical
. . . Newcomers always get stage fright . . . Another United Cigar store . . . Say, if they pro-
hibited smoking where would we find telephone
booths? . . . The Palace across the street . . . It
used to be the dream of all vaudevillians to play
there . . . Now if the movie houses don't get them,
they're there . . .

"And there's a crowd there lauding you and applaud-
ing you
When you're on top;
Same crowd hissing you and dismissing you
If you should flop . . ."

The photomatic . . . You take your own picture . . . Eight for a quarter . . . They're all
ready to take home in five minutes . . . Say, isn't
this a wonderful age? . . . Let's get tomorrow's
paper today and see what has happened tomorrow
. . . This age sure is great . . .

"But those who fail must learn to say
Tomorrow is another day . . ."

Here we are at Fifty-second Street . . . Just ten
blocks . . . It's dull from here up . . . Broadway's a small place, isn't it? . . . Just ten blocks

. . . Ten blocks for all the world to get famous in . . .

"That's Broadway, Broadway,
The Heart of the World. . . ."

HE has a name that will live forever and he bought it for a song. IRVING BERLIN.

Came to this country at the age of four, the youngest of eight children. In Russia his father was a cantor. Here a kosher butcher.

He has yet to find a hat to fit him.

He eats a lot for one of his size.

Plays the piano by ear. And only in F sharp. Has a specially constructed piano with a sliding keyboard. When the music calls for another key he merely moves the lever.

He is not a one finger player. Uses all his fingers badly.

Has a scar on his forehead. It was received on a Washington's Birthday in Cherry Street, trying to start a bonfire.

Thinks he is a good stud poker player. His friends say he's lucky.

His pet aversions are riveters and second verses.

Ran away from home at the age of fourteen. His first stop was Callahan's saloon. Here he sang "The Mansion of Aching Hearts" until enough coins were tossed at him to pay for a night's lodging. Later became a singing waiter at Nigger Mike's place, 12 Pell Street. The barker on the trip to Chinatown bus now points out the place.

He wrote "Alexander's Ragtime Band," credited with starting the jazz vogue, at the age of twenty-three.

Crowds frighten him. So do certain individuals.

His idea of a great achievement is writing a song that reaches the million copy mark.

Maintains a home in West Forty-sixth Street. But lives elsewhere. The first of every month generally finds him moving.

His square monicker is Israel Baline. For a time he went under the name of Cooney. Became Berlin because that was the way the Bowery pronounced Baline.

As a singing waiter he kicked a hoofer named George White out of the place for being a pest, and also served Al Smith.

Is always chewing gum. This can be observed by merely watching the funny way his hat moves on his head.

His favorite biographer is Alexander Woollcott.

He composes in this fashion: First playing the song on the piano. Then singing it to Arthur Johnson, his right and left hand man, who records upon paper what he hears. Then Johnson plays the written manuscript. This is the first draft. From this

78

Berlin works on to the final version. Often after a song has been published he changes it.

His bill for flowers for the Mrs. is $1,000 a month.

His patent leather dinner shoes have more cracks than his hair has waves.

Of all the songs he has written, a figure exceeding four hundred, his favorite is "The Song Is Ended But the Melody Lingers On."

Is very restless. Can't sit or stand still. Always paces the floor. He walks miles in any room he is in. It is the only exercise he gets.

As far as playwrights go, his taste begins and ends with George S. Kaufman. As for music, he'll whistle anything by Jerome Kern. For lyrics he hands first prize to B. G. De Sylva. And if asked to name the swellest guy in the theatrical game, he'd shout Sam Harris.

He has had to change his entire working schedule since he became a father.

He has never worn a diamond. The only jewelry he wears is, occasionally, a pearl tie pin.

Never eats the crust of bread or rolls. Always plucks the filling. This can be seen circled about his plate.

After finishing a song he sings it to the first person he meets. A bell boy at Palm Beach was the first to hear "Lazy." A Broadway taxi driver was the first to hear "All Alone." A bewildered stranger, occupation unknown, was the first to hear "Say It With Music."

He never writes anything in longhand but his signature on a check. Everything else he prints.

The one thing in life he is looking forward to is walking into a restaurant with his daughter, Mary Ellen.

Of all the songs ever written the one he'd love to be the author of is "The Rosary."

On the fly leaf of a book containing every song he wrote there is this ditty which he believes sums up everything:

> *Let Me Be a Troubadour,*
> *And I Will Ask For Nothing More*
> *Than One Short Hour Or So,*
> *To Sing My Song And Go.*

He has a form-fitting couch which was especially designed for him.

SOME people write one play and then are never heard from again. But this fellow's inexhaustible. OWEN DAVIS.

He is a tiptop cook.

There never will be an exact count of how many plays he wrote. He wrote at least three hundred. Between the ages of twenty-seven and forty he remembers nothing but writing plays. Somehow, between scripts, he managed to get married. Also to raise a family. Didn't notice either until he was forty. Then took up golf.

He knows much more about a lot of theatrical managers than they care to have him know.

Had a unique contract with A. H. Woods. It stated that for a period of five years he could write plays for Woods only. Also stated that during that period Woods couldn't produce any plays but his. During those years he wrote fifty-eight melodramas, or a play a month for five years.

He'd go to Europe tomorrow if they'd build a railroad across the Atlantic Ocean.

He doesn't drink. He'd like to.

Is a Harvard graduate. Played football on the

Crimson eleven. Also held that college's record for the hundred-yard dash until four years ago.

In those days of the thrilling melodramas Woods would select a title and order terrifying lithographs of maidens in peril. Then Davis would write a play to fit both the title and the picture.

Perhaps you recall some of them. They include such titles as *Through the Breakers, Deadwood Dick's Last Shot, The Chinatown Trunk Mystery, Confessions of a Wife, The Gambler From the West, Tony the Bootblack, The Great Express Robbery, Queen of the Opium Ring, Convict 999, Broadway After Dark, The Policeman and the Millionaire's Wife, The Creole Slave's Revenge, A Chorus Girl's Luck in New York,* and *Edna, the Pretty Typewriter.*

He doesn't remember writing *Bertha, the Sewing Machine Girl,* although he is credited with it.

His play *Icebound* won the 1923 Pulitzer prize. *The Detour* he considers his greatest play.

Always smokes cigars. At rehearsals he makes a little cup from a newspaper to flick his ashes in. He is well house broken.

Clarence Darrow is his idea of the greatest American.

Prefers the theater to the movies, ices to ice cream, a four-in-hand to a bow tie, a cold bath to a hot one, poker to bridge and a wicked woman to a simple one.

The first theatrical flashlight ever made was of

his play *The Road to Paradise*. It is now pasted on the wall of his workroom. Among those in it are Mrs. Davis, then the "You Ain't Done Right by Our Nell" girl. And George Jessel's stepmother, then very interested in keeping the villian from foreclosing on the old homestead.

Wrote his first play, *The Rival Detectives,* at the age of eight. All the characters in it were murdered.

His ambition is to have a perfect script after the first writing. Thought he had it with *The Nervous Wreck.* Then had to rewrite it seven times.

Once was turning out so many plays that he had to write under seven different names. Two of the nom de plumes, Robert Wayne and John Oliver, became well known. In fact, a Pittsburgh dramatic critic wrote a piece about John Oliver stating that "at last a man had come along to drive Owen Davis out of business."

Eugene O'Neill is his favorite playwright.

When writing he moods himself to the play. While working on *Chinatown Charlie* he lived on chop suey.

The first wedding he ever attended was his own.

Give him a hundred hours and he'll have a play written, cast and ready for rehearsal. *The Donovan Affair* took a week to write; *The Detour* a month; *Icebound* a year; *Chinatown Charlie* an hour. He wrote nine third acts for *To-night at Twelve* on the train to Atlantic City.

The only army he'd fight for is the Salvation Army.

When it comes to humorists he hands first prize to Frank Sullivan.

Every opening night he hangs about the lobby listening to the comment. If it is unfavorable he hurries home, and before the reviews have been published he is at work on another play.

In the beginning he took criticism seriously. He knocked out the critic—and with one punch—who panned his first production.

Is a tremendous pie eater. Every morning for breakfast he has two kinds of pie.

While working for a prominent picture concern, that company sent a form letter to all their authors and stars saying that a ten per cent reduction of salaries was going into effect. They hoped that this reduction would be approved by all those who really loved the movies. Why, even the executives had agreed. To this charming letter Mr. Davis replied: "I appreciate your sentiment in taking a reduction because you love the movies. As for myself, however, I must beg you to continue my contract because I hate the damn pictures."

He is tone deaf.

His first play he submitted to the Charles Frohman office. Charles Klein, author of *The Lion and the Mouse*, was the playreader then. After reading the play he said: "You look like a strong man." Davis proudly replied that he was. "Well, then," said Klein, "take this masterpiece and throw it as far as you can, and never write another."

There's always a woman in the case. And the Theatre Guild has Helen Westley.

Her full name is Henrietta Remsen Meserole Westley. She comes from a clan of prim old Huguenots. Two streets in Brooklyn, Remsen and Meserole, are named after her ancestors.

Is downhearted because men look upon her in a motherly fashion.

For years her stage was the back room of Greenwich Village cafés and bookstores. She wandered in, strutted her stuff and wandered out—a will-o'-the-wisp. One evening a group of intellectuals planned to start a theater. This little elf entered and this time she didn't leave. Today she's a trade-mark.

Her passion is reading subtitles aloud. Talking pictures annoy her.

She believes in God and is a member of the Dutch Reformed Church.

Claims she is a good luck piece of the Guild. Must have a hand in everything they do. She played in both *Strange Interlude* and *Faust* the same evening. Merely left one play about the third act, hurried down the street with makeup on and went on in the other.

89

Her purse is large enough to pass as baggage at any hotel. It always contains a mess of bills, cosmetics, letters, keys, bric-a-brac and ashes.

Flowers, she thinks, are horrid. Her summer home, a shack at Croton, is surrounded by weeds.

Haunts second-hand stores. She detests breaking in new garments. Her shoes are one size too large. At present she is wearing a cane.

Likes to use big words in conversation. The listener generally doesn't know what they mean.

She never gets peeved. Is always quaint.

Adores babies and makes special visits just to pinch their cheeks. She has a gentle pinch.

Went to Paris once. Drank milk of magnesia all the way over so she wouldn't get seasick. Stayed eleven days and never went outside of Montmartre.

Envies Heywood Brown for his ability to dress better.

The only restaurant she ever liked she found in Chicago. Raved about it for five months. Then arranged a supper party there. Paying the railroad fare of four guests. Arriving, she learned the restaurant had been closed by the Health Department.

Studies Yoga philosophy.

Belongs to over twenty freak societies. With the hope that some day one of them might amount to something.

Calls upon her friends without notice. And whenever the desire seizes her. Regardless of the time.

Thinks nothing of returning a book at three in the morning.

She buys costumes from old Theatre Guild plays and uses them for street clothes.

Her most precious possession is a jade necklace. Whenever she gets another piece she adds it to the necklace. It now hangs about her knees.

Before her daughter, Ethel Westley, was born she attended the Metropolitan Opera House and visited the art museums weekly so the child would be artistic.

She claims she was the first modern woman.

Traffic doesn't bother her. When wishing to cross a congested avenue in a hurry she merely lets out a terrific shriek. People as well as autos stop.

She feels she should know more policemen.

Goes for long walks with a bottle of milk under her arm and feeds stray cats. While on these journeys she also buys liver for dogs. The delicatessen store near the Guild Theatre has a standing order to feed all stray cats and charge it to her milk fund.

Thinks the North was right in the civil war.

When her daughter was to be married the entire Theatre Guild acting company asked her what Ethel would like for a wedding gift. She replied: "Ethel is very fond of coffee pots." Ethel received thirty-eight coffee pots.

She groans when she walks up a flight of stairs.

She washes herself with oil.

THE 1929 Pulitzer prize play winner: ELMER L. RICE. He was born September 28, 1892. The locale: Madison Avenue near 106th Street. Until he was twenty-six he lived within a radius of two miles of his birthplace.

He has red hair. Shaves at least once a day. However, he has to be told to take a haircut.

He likes to go for long walks, wander through museums and look out of windows.

Graduated from public school. Went halfway through high school. He has no recollection of learning anything there of value to him. Later studied law. When he was admitted to the bar he quit the profession.

He is married and has two children—Robert, aged twelve, and Margaret, aged nine.

Hates to get up in the morning. His friends know enough never to disturb him before ten-thirty.

When he finished writing *Street Scene* he was critically ill. His wife peddled the play, bringing it first to the Theatre Guild. They rejected it and so did John Golden, Jed Harris and Arthur Hopkins. The news that *Street Scene* had been rejected by these producers was kept from Rice until he recovered from his illness. An agent sold the play to William A. Brady.

He has never been to a night club and never intends going.

Doesn't care for the theater. He attends about three times a year and then sees musical comedies. Recently, because he has to cast two plays next season, he has been going to the theater three or four times a week. He has yet to see the third act of a play this year.

His name was Elmer L. Reizenstein. The L is for Leopold.

He owns some bum oil stocks.

The first time he ever went to the theater was when he was eighteen years old. Three years later he wrote his first play. It was *On Trial*. Similar to *Street Scene*, it was rejected by almost every producer, and then was a big hit when finally produced by Arthur Hopkins. William A. Brady was one of the many who rejected it.

Is especially fond of fat German pretzels and beer.

Writes his plays in longhand. Then gives them to his secretary to type. He hates to rewrite and seldom does. It took him three months to write *Street Scene*.

He is not interested in baseball, football or boxing. He never plays golf or bridge. Occasionally he goes to the race track, but he never bets.

One of his great joys is reading poetry aloud to his kiddies.

He is lazy. His motto is: "Never put off doing tomorrow what you can put off doing until the day after tomorrow." Once he starts, however, he works intensely, often for ten hours at a stretch.

The most tragic event in his life was when, at the age of eight, he proudly walked out of the house wearing his first derby hat only to have it and himself beaten up by the rough boys of the district.

He doesn't talk much.

He lives in a hotel. He loathes home-cooked meals and always eats in a restaurant.

Some of the other plays he has written are *The Home of the Free*, *For the Defense*, *The Iron Cross*, *Wake Up, Jonathan* (written with Hatcher Hughes), *It Is the Law* (written with Hayden Talbot), *The Adding Machine*, *Close Harmony* (written with Dorothy Parker), *The Mongrel*, *Cock Robin* (written with Philip Barry) and *The Subway*.

He has never voted.

His pet hate is the movies. Believes that they have no future. He once worked in Hollywood for two years. He wrote *Doubling for Romeo*, the picture in which Will Rogers appeared.

The set used in *Street Scene* is an exact copy of 25 West Sixty-fifth Street.

He would rather live in Naples than any other place in the world.

His lawyer when selling the movie rights to *On Trial*, twelve years ago, inserted a clause in the contract that the talking picture rights were to remain the property of the author. The movie magnate, who didn't know what talking pictures were, readily agreed to this condition. Recently, Rice sold the talking picture rights to *On Trial* for a huge sum.

His hobby is painting with water colors.

When he wrote *Cock Robin* with Philip Barry, the collaboration was done entirely by mail. They exchanged drafts of the acts until both were suited. The authors never saw each other until the play was completed.

He never puts sugar in his coffee.

He learned that he had won the Pulitzer Prize a week before the official announcement. Of course there was much joy and excitement in the Rice household. Not wanting the news to get out, he pledged everyone to secrecy. However, he was a little afraid that his son, Robert, would boast about the prize to his schoolmates. He called Robert aside and warned him privately. Robert listened attentively and then replied, "Who wants to know, anyway?"

He hates Broadway. He thinks it is the cheapest place in the world.

EDDIE CANTOR. His name isn't Eddie and it isn't
Cantor. It's Izzy Iskowitch.

He never saw his mother or father.

Although a bundle of nerves and energy on the
stage, he is very quiet at home. Likes to sit around in
pajamas and rest.

His theatrical career started as a singing usher in
a movie house. Also was in Gus Edwards's "Kid Kab-
aret" act. Then he joined Bedini and Arthur, a
noted team of jugglers. He brought them articles
to juggle. Later he became half of the vaudeville
team of "Cantor and Lee."

When working before a microphone or making a
record he feels depressed because an audience can't
see his eyes.

Was once an errand boy for the Isaac Gellis Wurst
Works.

His birthday, if you're interested, is January 31.
He was born in 1892 on Eldridge Street, New York.
His great hobby in life is maintaining the Surprise
Lake Camp for boys of the East Side. Who, like him-
self when a youth, never get any air and sunshine.

First started his peppy style of racing up stage

and down in 1910 singing a song called "The Rag-time Violin" written by a new song-writer named Irving Berlin.

Enjoys boxing with people. Often in his dressing room when a male visitor enters he will spar with him. He would like to be a strong man.

The dream of his life for many years was to build his own home. While the house was being completed he was thinking of selling it.

He is a good business man and quick to sense an opportunity. Wall Street had no sooner crashed than he had written a book called, *Caught Short*. Even in his dressing room he is business-like, having a secretary, a desk and a telephone.

The first play he ever saw was *The Talk Of New York* by George M. Cohan, starring Victor Moore, at the Grand Opera House, Twenty-third Street and Eighth Avenue.

He has his clothes made by Mayor Walker's tailor.

Is fussy about food. Eats with an eye to calories and vitamines. Every so often, however, he falls off the wagon and goes in for a heavy kosher meal which he loves.

His two favorite games are ping-pong and casino. He is a swell casino player.

The first play he ever appeared in was *Canary Cottage*, written by Earl Carroll.

Is always running to a doctor for something or other. One day a doctor examined him and said:

"There's something wrong with a gland in your throat. That's the reason your eyes bulge. But I'm happy to say that I can cure you." Cantor looked at the doctor and before racing from his office said: "You don't fix that gland. I should pay you yet to take away my livelihood. No, sir! Good-bye!"

He would like to be the founder of a new religion.

Is a hard worker on the stage. When he was in the last *Follies* he said to a friend: "Drop around any time. I'm always on."

In his new home which he calls, "The House That Ziegfeld's Jack Built," the bathroom contains every type of a shower. He is able to take a shower standing, sitting, leaning or reclining.

He hates bad wine, bad women and bad songs. Especially bad songs.

Has a passion for hats. His dressing room is generally crowded with special made headwear both for street use and for comedy purposes.

The ambition of his life is to be the father of a boy. He has five daughters. They are Marjorie, Natalie, Edna, Marilyn and Janet. Marjorie and Natalie were named after relatives. Edna, because it was a pretty name. Marilyn was named after Marilyn Miller. Janet was named after the nurse.

After his fifth daughter was born one wit wisecracked: "Cantor is trying to raise his own Albertina Rasch ballet."

In his home he has a special room where he keeps copies of *My Life Is In Your Hands.*

He has only one mark on his body. It is a scar on his forehead, a result of his wild childhood days.

Although he is worth two million dollars, his signature on a check isn't worth a penny. His checks must be signed by Dan Lipsky who is his proxy for life.

In his book, *My Life Is In Your Hands,* he remembers the story of his life from two years before he was born.

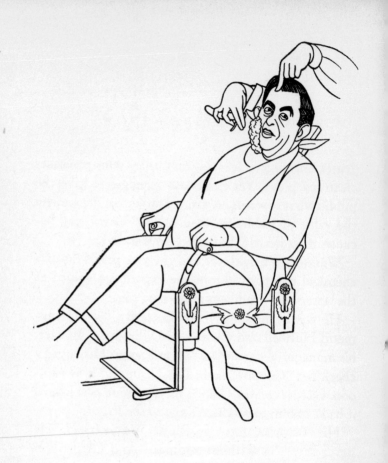

JOHN GOLDEN. He's the only man who produces clean sex plays. Yet he always manages to give the public what it wants. A shrewd showman, he realizes the value of publicity. Started the "clean" gag because of its healthy box office appeal. It has "it."

Was once a bricklayer and the vice president of a chemical company. From the experience gained at the latter he is proficient at making gin.

He wrote the song "Poor Butterfly," with Raymond Hubbell and Charles B. Dillingham. In fact, his managerial career started on a song. His royalty check for "Goodby, Girls, I'm Through," was $40,-000. Gave it to Mrs. Golden for a present. She loaned it back to him to produce *Turn to the Right*.

His favorite actor is Muni Weisenfrend. He never says this without adding: "And Otto Kahn agrees with me."

Is very much interested in what makes an audience go to a play. Once distributed a circular during the run of *Pigs* inquiring, "What made you attend this show?" Seventy per cent of the answers were variations of "Because a friend told me about it."

As a bricklayer he helped build the Garrick Theatre.

For the last thirty years the annual Lambs' Washing has been held on his estate at Bayside.

He was a partner of Cohan and Harris in the production of *Hawthorne of the U. S. A.* His task was to pal about with Douglas Fairbanks, seeing that the young acrobat didn't hurdle over taxicabs and climb up buildings.

He is superstitious. Likes to have a numeral in the title of his plays. Remember: *The 1st Year, 2 Girls Wanted, 3 Wise Fools, 4 Walls* and *7th Heaven.* Considers 27 his lucky number. In roulette and other numerical games of chance he will bet huge amounts on it.

He organized the Producing Managers Association. This led to the famous actors' strike.

The man he quotes most is Ring Lardner.

Is not fussy about clothing. Never goes to a store to purchase wearing apparel. If he needs another tie, shirt or suit, he merely telephones for it.

Thinks Atlantic City and Miami are the only vacation spots worth knowing.

He is one of the few producers who treat the theater as if it were a business. Is in his office by nine every morning and leaves at five. Is in bed every night at ten. He never attends the theater in the evenings. Goes only to matinées. Misses every opening night. Even his own.

Owns the original Old Kentucky Home, having

bought the Stephen Foster homestead in Federal Hill to save it from being torn down.

He realizes the value of flattery. Gets the most out of people he is associated with by using it.

His favorite tryout town is Elmira, N. Y. Believes it to be lucky and opens all his shows there.

Was the first to cover the front of a theater with an electric sign. Did it with *3 Wise Fools* at the Criterion. Then the movies took up the idea. . . . And how!

He hates the word "clean." Refrains from using it in his conversation. When it slips out accidentally, he looks embarrassed.

He has collaborated on songs with Irving Berlin, Douglas Fairbanks, Oscar Hammerstein, Victor Herbert and Woodrow Wilson.

Always puts on his glasses when he talks on the telephone.

His hobby is collecting "the key to the city." He has framed in his office keys to twenty-seven of the most important cities in the United States.

He hates dogs and cringes when he sees one.

Has a barber shop in his office, fully equipped. Every day at twelve a barber appears and shaves him. Every other week he takes a haircut.

His home in Bayside has eight bedrooms. He sleeps in a different room each night, according to his mood.

PAUL WHITEMAN. Let the most important fact come first. He weighs 248 pounds.

He once studied to be a mechanical engineer.

He has a passion for striped ties and flashy autos.

Was born in Denver, March 28, 1890. His father and mother were both six feet tall. His father was director of musical education in the city schools. His mother sang in the choir.

Once he enlisted in the navy. Then he organized a naval jazz band.

His prize possession is a photograph of himself at the age of three. Here he is seen wearing green velvet pants and playing a toy violin.

He can lead an orchestra by merely shrugging his shoulders or moving his thumbs.

Was a viola player in the Denver Symphony Orchestra and drove a taxi on the side to make money.

Custard is his favorite dessert. He calls it "gap and swallow."

The Prince of Wales is his pal.

He is married to Vanda Hoff, dancer. They have a son, Paul Whiteman, Junior.

One of his first jobs in a jazz band was in a

honky-tonk in San Francisco. Here the folks threw coins in a barrel if they liked you. These coins were your salary.

He plays golf and has one friend he can beat.

Will pay any price for a musician he desires. Often takes men getting only $60 a week away from another band by paying them $250 a week.

Made his New York début at the Palais Royal.

The first place that he heard jazz was at Capper's Neptune Palace in Africa.

Has a remarkable memory, never forgetting the smallest detail. Commenting on this trait, a wisecracker gagged: "Oh, well, an elephant never forgets."

Never passes a street musician without slipping him a bill.

Whenever he attends the opera he cries. His favorite opera is *Parsifal*.

For relaxation he will sit before a victrola listening to records of his band playing.

Eats very little for one of his size. Some of his choice dishes are chicken and cream as served at the Claypool Hotel, Indianapolis; hot cakes, doughnuts and strawberry shortcake at his relatives' in Denver; wienerwurst and sauerkraut at Joe's in Minneapolis and antipasto at Sardi's.

The first record he ever made was "Avalon." It was spoiled in repeated trials by the audible soft oaths of players cursing their own mistakes.

The first of the Whitemans spelled it Wightman.

He wears pink nightgowns that fall to his an-
kles, and a tasseled night cap.

Studied with one teacher for four years. Then
hired another teacher who spent four years teach-
ing him not to do the things the first one had told
him to do.

He can't eat unless someone is sitting at the table
with him.

Ferde Grofe makes the orchestrations for him.
Grofe orchestrated "The Song of India" and "The
Rhapsody in Blue" for him. These were the first
pieces of jazz to be heard in Aeolian Hall.

Amuses himself at home by playing with toy lo-
comotives.

His chief means of income in the old days was
playing at parties for Ehret, the brewer. Got $1,000
a party.

Is sentimental and shy. Whenever a chorus girl
tells him that she loves him (and it happens) he
blushes profusely.

The dream of his life is to retire and spend the
rest of his days on his 250-acre ranch near Denver.

He gets crying jags.

Lindbergh made the first non-stop flight to Paris,
but everlasting fame still awaits the aviator who
makes the first nonstop flight around Paul Whiteman. This is his own joke.

Talks to his band in pig Latin, a language he speaks fluently.

Likes to sit in his roadster parked near the stage door of the theater he is playing and hear the passers-by say: "Oh, look, there's Paul Whiteman."

He perspires freely. When rehearsing he discards his coat, vest, tie, and unbuttons his shirt. Always wears an old golf cap turned backward. Usually it takes him forty minutes to rehearse a number.

Is a hypochondriac. Whenever he goes on the road he takes a doctor with him.

When any member of his band is late for rehearsal he is fined. The man who has paid the most fines is Paul Whiteman.

Tells amusing parlor car stories somewhat in the literary manner of James Branch Cabell.

He was once fired from Taits, a San Francisco restaurant, because he couldn't possibly play jazz.

Every Christmas he throws a party which never costs less than $3,000 and never breaks up until it is time for breakfast.

His hobby is collecting hotel signs. The prize of his collection is one that he picked up in Arizona. It reads: "Women—Do Not Take Men to Your Rooms. Ladies Will Not."

While making the picture, "The King of Jazz," he staggered on the set and said: "I've just had a full night's sleep. It's the first time in years and it darn near killed me."

Although he may occasionally bawl out his men in a deep basso voice, he always uses baby talk to his wife.

"NEVER GIVE A SUCKER AN EVEN BREAK"

W. C. FIELDS. His real name is William Claude Duganfield.

He can't rehearse his part in a play or picture without holding a cane in his hand.

His auto bears a California license plate merely because he likes the color of it.

Started his theatrical career as a juggler. At the enormous salary of $5 a week. Out of this he had to pay an agent a dollar and a half commission fee. His latest salary was $5,500 weekly as the star of the Earl Carroll *Vanities*. The agent's making more also.

He wears snake-skin shoes. Never wears garters. Calls his socks, "droopies."

Is an excellent caricaturist and could probably earn a living by drawing if he so desired.

Good comedy, he believes, is merely a matter of instinct.

He traveled around the world twice. Once making the westward passage. The other time the eastern passage. To him one of life's little mysteries is why they lost or gained a day on the way around.

Wears silk underwear and sleeps in it. Sleeps lying flat on his belly with the pillow against his chest.

One of his first jobs in the theater was in a beer garden, the Fortesque Pavilion, Atlantic City. His task was to go in swimming and cry for help. Then two actors would rush to his aid, carry him back to the beer garden and revive him on the stage there. While this revival act was going on the waiters would sell beers to the crowd that had followed the drowning man to the pavilion.

Washes himself with black tar soap. Perfumes his bath with pine needles.

Is always juggling things by force of habit. Has six lemons on his bureau at home. When alone he amuses himself by juggling them.

Thinks the best French food is served in England. The best German food in America. And as far as American food is concerned he'd rather eat tall grass.

His nickname is "Pokey."

He ran away from home at the age of eleven and became a hobo.

During his hobo career he was regarded as a Beau Brummell, because he washed once a day.

He made the longest jump on record. Jumped from Freemantle, Australia, traveling thirty-eight days and thirty-eight nights, to play a one-night stand in Syracuse, N. Y.

His two favorite expressions, which he made

popular, are: "It ain't a fit night for man nor beast" and "Never give a sucker an even break."

He has a face that caricaturists love.

The thing that annoys him most in life is a radio. When entering a house that has one, he politely requests that it be turned off. He owns two radios. Has one in his dressing room. The other at home. They are to amuse his guests when he isn't present.

He once passed the night in an Egyptian pyramid.

Recently he received a letter from the United States Government about his income tax. He had overpaid it $1,250.

He eats only one meal a day. Never has breakfast or lunch. Only dinner. Occasionally, however, after the theater, he will have cheese, crackers and beer.

No matter how hard he tries he can't raise a mustache. Has over a hundred false mustaches as part of his theatrical makeup. He wears the mustache, not on his lip, but on the tip of his nose. They have a trick clasp.

His favorite actor is Mussolini.

Among the things that burn him up and leave him cold are mustard, folks who get plastered on one highball, picnics, hand-embroidered handkerchiefs, chorus girls with curls, "Mammy" singers with Jewish accents and a pair of tight pants.

He played the stock market once. Then he

bought five shares of stock on a tip. Almost went into a panic the next day when he couldn't find the stock listed.

He once saved his life by juggling before a wild tribe in Africa.

He never smokes. Except when rehearsing a show or making a picture. Then he is an inveterate smoker, lighting one cigarette with the butt of another.

Like John Held, Jr., his library is in his bathroom.

While in Hollywood making pictures he received a broken neck. Today he can only turn his neck halfway to the left. He can, however, make a complete right turn.

He is the possessor of a Phi Beta Kappa key which he found.

SOME people achieve fame by playing the piano. But this little lady got that way by sitting on one. HELEN MORGAN.

She never uses perfume.

Her favorite colors are black and flame red.

She was born in Danville, Ill. Uncle Joe Cannon's home town. When a baby he used to tickle her under the chin.

Her first job was as a cash girl in Marshall Field's. Later was a telephone operator and a model. She attended twenty-six schools and finally managed to graduate from public school.

Can cook and sew but can't knit. Used to cook when her mother took in boarders while they lived in Chicago. Her mother was a Sunday school teacher.

The only flower she will wear is the camellia. Her life ambition is to play *Camille*.

Once won a beauty contest as "Miss Montreal." Much to the embarrassment of the judges who later discovered that she had been living only three weeks in Montreal. In New York she was received by the Mayor and crowned the "Miss 1925."

Buys at least four dresses a week. Often purchases a hundred pairs of stockings at one time. Always takes a man with her when she goes shopping.

Was discovered by Amy Leslie, critic of the Chicago *Daily News*. Miss Leslie brought her to Florenz Ziegfeld who gave her an audition. He placed her in the chorus of *Sally*, then on the road.

Her next dealing with Ziegfeld was some years later when, without having ever seen her work, he signed her to play in *Show Boat*. She was in Europe at the time.

She is crazy about mice. Has two live white mice for pets. Her stationery is monogrammed with a mouse. Her nickname is "Mousey."

She rouges her lips between kisses.

First sat on a piano when working in The Backstage Club. The reason she took to sitting on a piano was because the night club was so crowded that it was the only place she could sit.

Once she adopted a baby. Only to have the mother, a chorus girl, kidnap it from her two months later.

Her favorite dish is potato soup as made by herself. It is made of potatoes with lots of cream and onions.

Likes to dress in men's clothing. Often works about the house in overalls. She sleeps in fancy colored men's pajamas. Sleeps with her head resting on so many pillows that she looks as if she were sitting up in bed.

Some years ago she appeared in a dramatic sketch with the Grand Guignol Players under the name of Neleh Nagrom. Which is her name spelled backwards.

When she sings, "Why Was I Born," she actually cries. Because she says she feels sorry for herself.

Reads all current novels. Her favorite author is Ernest Hemingway. She owns a copy of James Joyce's *Ulysses* which was punctuated especially for her.

Is shy about exposing her body. Wouldn't let her mother see her in *Americana* because she had to wear short panties in a dance number.

Necklaces and bracelets annoy her. Earrings give her a headache. The only jewelry she wears is a love altar. This was given to her by a titled Englishman who wanted to marry her.

She dislikes hearing her own phonograph records. At parties, when anyone plays them, she gets up and breaks them.

Always has her hair cut by the same barber. The coiffure is now known as the "Helen Morgan Haircut." She combs her hair carefully. So as to make it look as if it hadn't been combed.

Her most valued possession is a pitcher that an Atlantic and Pacific grocery store gave her in return for coupons when she was a kid.

The minute she enters a house she loosens her garters and walks about with her stockings hanging over the top of her shoes.

Is popular and very much sought after. But generally not by the man she likes. When singing, "Someday He'll Come Along, The Man I Love," she means it.

She is fond of pets. Has two love birds, a dog named Mose, and one goldfish—the other died. She had two baby alligators. She kept them in the bathtub. Had to give them away because they snapped at her toes when she took shower baths.

Often wears only a kimono, with a fur coat over it, when driving to the theater in her roadster.

She corresponds with William S. Hart regularly. This started after Bill Hart heard her sing, "My Bill." He took it rather personally.

She has a possum claw birthmark on her right ankle.

If she were a man she'd be a sailor.

EUGENE O'NEILL. He is the only Broadway playwright who was born in Times Square. He was born
in the Barrett House, now the Hotel Cadillac, at
Forty-third Street and Broadway. The date: October 16, 1888.

He always wears dark clothes.

When writing he uses either pen and ink or a
typewriter. It merely depends on which is handy.
Revising a play annoys him.

His father was James O'Neill—an actor famous
for his portrayal of the Count of Monte Cristo.
Her mother, a fine pianist, attended a convent with
the mother of George Jean Nathan.

He's a great swimmer and doesn't mind cold
water.

Night life doesn't appeal to him. He made one
tour of the night clubs. It was his last.

Never attends the opening of his plays. In fact
he seldom goes to a theater. He'd rather read a play
than see it performed.

While at Provincetown, a feeble-minded lad of
six took a great liking to him. One day while sitting
on the beach the boy asked: "What is beyond the

Point? What is beyond the sea? What is beyond Europe?" O'Neill answered, "The horizon." "But," persisted the boy, "what is beyond the horizon?"

Could grow a beard in ten days if he didn't shave.

His father, who said he never would be a great playwright, lived to see his son's first great success, *Beyond the Horizon*.

He hasn't touched a drop of liquor in the last three years.

In his youth Jack London, Joseph Conrad and Rudyard Kipling were his favorite authors. Today Nietzsche is his literary idol.

He can't walk a mile without meeting an old friend who asks for money. He gives.

After the opening of *Strange Interlude* he chanced to meet an old seafaring friend. O'Neill asked what he was doing, and the friend replied: "Oh, I've married and settled down. Got a nice little business and doing pretty good. And you, Gene, are you still working the boats?"

Reads all the reviews of his plays. He claims he knows the good critics from the bad ones.

He seldom talks unless he has something to say.

While writing he hates to be disturbed. When working at Provincetown he tacked this sign outside his door: "Go to hell."

Is crazy about prize fights and the six-day bicycle races. When in town he will go to anything at Madison Square Garden. The only person he ever expressed a desire to meet was Tex Rickard.

His full name is Eugene Gladstone O'Neill. Lately he discarded the middle name entirely.

Once, when a mere infant, he was very ill in Chicago. George Tyler, then his father's manager, ran about the streets of that city at three in the morning for a doctor.

Is always making notes for future plays. He wrote the notes of his first plays in the memorandum section of that grand publication, *The Bartender's Guide*.

He likes to be alone.

He had three favorite haunts. One was Jimmy the Priest's saloon, a waterfront dive. He later made use of this locale in *Anna Christie*. Another was "Hell's Hole," a Greenwich Village restaurant. The third was the Old Garden Hotel, which was situated on the northeast corner of Madison Avenue and Twenty-seventh Street. Here he met many people of the sporting world. A former bicycle rider (now a megaphone shouter on a sightseeing bus) he met there is still a pal of his.

It took him three years to write *Strange Interlude*. He had only six of the nine acts completed when he sold the play to the Theatre Guild.

He is especially fond of fine linen.

When in New York he lives at a secondary hotel. A place no one would ever think of looking for him.

He has huge hands.

For every play he draws sketches suggesting designs for the sets.

Of his own work he prefers, *The Hairy Ape*, *The Straw* (this he considers the best of his naturalistic plays), *Marco Millions*, *Strange Interlude* and *Lazarus Laughed*. The last is to be produced next year by the Moscow Art Theatre.

He takes great delight in recounting droll stories. Tells them with feeling and skill.

While attending Professor Baker's class at Harvard he almost ruined the college careers of John Colton and Johnny Weaver by filling them full of beer.

Is now living in France. He does not intend to return to America for some years.

His first book, *Thirst and Other One-Act Plays*, was published at his expense.

All of his original manuscripts are in his possession despite offers in five figures for them.

He writes important messages which are not to be breathed to a soul, on the back of a postal card.

In Shanghai, on his recent trip around the world, he was called a faker posing as Eugene O'Neill.

William Shakespeare.—Was born April 22, 1564, in a little house on Henley Street, Stratford-on-Avon. The stunning event occurred at precisely three minutes past eight. His dad was already at work, not interested.

He was the third child. Since then he has written thirty-seven plays, five poems and one hundred and fifty-three sonnets. Since then people have advocated Birth Control.

Always wears Buster Brown collars, Windsor ties, knickers and silk stockings.

His favorite eating place is the Mermaid Tavern.

It's claimed that he steals his ideas. He doesn't deny it. Believes there's nothing new under the sun. Hopes that some day people will steal from him.

He is vain and conceited. His favorite topic is William Shakespeare. He can talk about him for hours.

He never uses the subway. Never listens to the radio. Never sends a telegram. Never telephones. He writes all his plays in longhand. He can't operate a typewriter.

Kit Marlowe and Ben Jonson he considers the

world's greatest men. His happiest moment was when he became the godfather of Jonson's son.

Started his theatrical career by holding horses outside the Globe Theatre. Later became an actor. Then wrote plays to make more money.

His favorite dish is olives.

He was a wild kid, up to all sorts of mischief. Often arrested for deer stealing. Left school at the age of thirteen. At the age of eighteen he had to marry Anne Hathaway. Six months later he became the father of an eight-pound baby, Susanna.

George Bernard Shaw thinks his stuff is piffle. He never heard of Shaw.

He talks with fluency in a high tenor voice. Has reddish hair, a pointed chin, a face that mirrors every change of emotion.

His main weakness is that he is overfond of sleep. No matter what time of day it is, or where he is, he can fall asleep at a moment's notice. He has never spent a sleepless night. Sleeps at least fourteen hours every day.

Rewrites all his stuff at least three times. Once rumored that Samuel Shipman was "ghost writing" his plays. This was discarded when critics proved that Shipman couldn't write that bad no matter how hard he tried.

He dislikes bacon.

Is gentle, gay and witty. His wisecracks generally get him into trouble. Because of one of his flippant

134

remarks he can't break into the movies. He said: "All the World's a Stage."

He can't carry his liquor. Two glasses of ale has him hugging the floor.

He refuses to allow Jed Harris to produce his play *Hamlet* because he doesn't want George Abbott to rewrite it.

He hobnobs with actors, stagehands and producers. Yet he is on intimate terms with Lord Pembroke, the Earl of Essex, the Earl of Southampton and the Prince of Wales.

He has made his will. In it he states that to his wife he leaves his second best bed.

His right ear is a little larger than his left. Says this is so because he sleeps on his right side.

His ambition is to write a play which the Theatre Guild will produce.

RELATIVELY SPEAKING

IN 1880 a wide-eyed immigrant walked down the gangplank of a steamship and stepped into America. His only possessions were fifty dollars and dreams. Today he wears eyeglasses and the shower in his office has gold faucets. His name was and still is CARL LAEMMLE.

He is stocky but only five feet in height. Is known as the smallest giant in the motion picture industry.

Was born in Laupheim, Germany. Today he owns the seal of the city.

Almost every important motion picture star has worked for him at some time or other.

He had left the clothing business. Was about to open a "five and ten cent store," when the crowds going into a nickelodeon attracted his attention. The man who formerly lectured on the fineness of buttonholes entered the motion picture business February 26, 1906. He opened the White Front movie house, admission five cents.

Is very kind and good-natured. In the middle of heart to heart talks, a favorite pastime with him, he always manages to say,"Isn't it a pity that we can't all be pleasant."

Is proud of the fact that he made the first million-dollar picture, *Foolish Wives*. While it was being made he had no idea it would cost that much.

His hobby and the distraction of all his associates is his wholesale importation of relatives and friends from Germany. They are immediately given jobs in the home office, Universal City and the various branches. It has been estimated that if he were to put them on a pension of a million dollars annually he would be saving a fortune.

He talks with a German accent but uses correct grammar.

Is always taking some medicine for some imaginary ailment. His doctor told him to walk for exercise. He does. But has his car trail him. After a two-block walk, he rides feeling just like an athlete.

He loves to be called "the old man" and "Uncle Carl."

He never personally breaks his promise.

In Universal City general managers are changed so rapidly that they are known as "the officers of the day."

His favorite eating places are Lindy's in New York and Henry's in Hollywood. Both are exactly alike. His happiest moments are spent there with a napkin tucked through the armholes of his vest and a plate of sauerbraten before him.

He never sits through an entire picture. Often

falls asleep in the projection room. Has a committee in New York who tell him about the pictures being made on the West Coast.

Is very proud of his home town. Makes all his employees donate their old clothes. Sends them to the poor people there. It's known as the Laemmle-Laupheim Fund.

The part of a picture that interests him most is the title. Will discuss the title and take suggestions from everybody, including the butcher boy.

He never meets a prominent person without having the cameras click.

Is a marvel with figures. Can tell you offhand how much they did in Siam the second week four years ago on any picture.

Has a special book in his office in which he makes his employees write what they think of him.

At the organization meeting nearly everyone wanted his name to be the name of the film company. Somewhat disgusted, he looked out of the window. Saw a white horse pulling a wagon labeled "Universal Pipe Fitting Company." He named it "The Universal Film Manufacturing Company."

His office must be larger than anyone else's. His desk is made to order so he can reach it. Sits with one leg dangling over the arm of a gros-point chair. The office contains polished mirrors, two-toned taffeta draperies and looks like a boudoir.

To show his patriotism during the war he produced *The Kaiser, the Beast of Berlin*. This picture provoked such bitter feeling in Germany that the next time he visited Laupheim he had to run out of the town in the middle of the night disguised as a woman.

The last person to have his ear is the party whose advice he follows.

A man tried to sell *My Sweetheart*, an old-time favorite play, to him for a talkie. "What kind of a play is it?" he asked.

"A pastoral drama," the man replied.

Laemmle thought for a moment and then said: "I don't think I can use that play. I don't like to put preachers in my pictures. It's bad for business."

He likes to wear red carnations in his lapel.

His greatest accomplishment was breaking the motion picture trust, making it possible for independents to produce.

Fought the trust for over two years. The day before the United States Supreme Court was to render the decision he was called out of town on business. Left word for his lawyer to let him know the result immediately. Elated over the victory the lawyer became dramatic and wired: "Justice Triumphs." To which Laemmle immediately wired back: "Appeal At Once."

PulEEZE!!!!

BEATRICE LILLIE was really born in Toronto, Canada. She went to England, alone, at the age of fifteen.

She likes anything that's green.

Her theatrical career started in *Charlot's Revue of 1915*. Here she made her first hit singing Irving Berlin's "I Want to Go Back to Michigan."

Has an inferiority complex whenever she talks business.

Her husband is Lord Peel. That makes her Lady Peel, in parentheses, to the rotogravure sections. Her supreme treasure is her son, Robert, who is here with her.

Is exactly the same offstage as she is on. Even says "Thank you" and "Puleeze" as she does for a laugh in the theater.

Sleeps perched up on three big pillows. Always has a sandwich placed on the night table and sleeps with socks on to keep her feet warm.

There are two things she really hates. One is to have her picture taken. The other is writing her signature.

She passed the blindfold test, endorsing a certain brand of cigarettes. She smokes an English cigarette called "Players." She endorsed Lux thinking it was candy.

She either likes a person at first sight or not at all.

As far as musical talent goes she can tickle a bit on the guitar.

The only legitimate play she ever appeared in was *Up in Mabel's Room*. It was a big hit here. It lasted six weeks in London. The critics said: "Beatrice Lillie played Beatrice Lillie very well."

A snowstorm fascinates her. During the snowstorms, while she was in this city, she went sleigh riding in Central Park.

Calls people "Ducky." If she doesn't call them "Ducky," she calls them "Chicken." Whenever something pleases her she refers to it as "A pretty kettle of fish."

Her son scolds her because she wears funny costumes on the stage. He believes she should always look pretty.

Among the things that make her shudder are people who chump hard candy, people who tell you they have a cold and then cough in your face to prove it, people who crack their knuckles and people who are always blowing bubbles with chewing gum.

She likes the saxophone because Lord Peel plays it.

She owns a dress suit. And wears it as well as she

144

does a Paris smock. *This Year of Grace* was the first show in her theatrical career in which she didn't wear it.

Every week she receives letters from people who want to sell her an old gun, an old piece of china or an old print that once belonged to the early Peels.

Almost everyone has his own nickname for her. Some of the most popular are: "Tiny," "Smally," "Beena," "Mina," "Hoyland," "Peanut," "Dumbell," "Crazy," "Oopie" and "Lady Peel."

She would rather visit a doctor than eat an apple. She only took a bite of the apple she is supposed to eat while singing "World Weary." This bite almost choked her.

She can name the horse the Prince of Wales didn't fall off.

Her favorite Americans are Robert Benchley, Donald Ogden Stewart, George S. Kaufman, Harold Ross, Marc Connolly and Alexander Woollcott. The Algonquin, she believes, is the capital of the United States.

Claims that no matter where she lives in this town of ours they are always building a house next to her bedroom. For this reason she sleeps with cotton in her ears.

Every evening she orders the same dinner. It consists of roast beef plain, plain boiled potatoes, plain white bread, Worcestershire sauce and plain spinach. She makes a special request that it be served by a plain waiter.

Her secret desire is to be able to speak with a Jewish accent.

Occasionally she gets a yen to talk to her husband in London. She puts the call in at one in the morning. At six she is awakened. London is on the phone. This is the conversation:

"Hello. How are you?"

"Very well. And you, sweetheart?"

"Great. How are the dogs?"

"They're fine. How's Robert?"

"Great. Oh—it just started to rain here."

"It's pretty foggy here."

"Good-by."

"Good-by."

And the bill was $187.

While out in Hollywood she was taken to the roof of a tall building by one of the natives, who pointed with pride to the city that lay below. And then he pointed to the sky and the stars above. "Beautiful, isn't it?" he asked. "Beautiful, but so artificial," replied Miss Lillie. "Some night I just know those stars will come together and spell Marion Davies."

Every morning before rising for breakfast she has a cup of tea in bed.

Once while walking along Fifth Avenue humming "The Cabman's Last Trip" a good-looking

chap tried to pick her up. She let him try for two
blocks and then took a taxi.

She always undresses in the bathroom. And lets
her clothes flop into the bathtub.

She once autographed a soldier's wooden leg.

THE ENGLISHMAN FROM AMERICA

LESLIE HOWARD. He so conquered this nation that in his native country, England, they refer to him as "that American actor."

He is nearsighted and wears glasses at all times, except when acting and reading.

His father was a stock broker. When he was graduated from Dulwich School, London, he had to work as a clerk in a bank. When the war broke out he joined the army to escape from this existence.

Never eats any meat because he dislikes eating animals. Eggs are his favorite dish. He often eats eggs three times a day.

Was "invalided" out of the army in 1918. Later that year he made his London theatrical début in Pinero's play *The Freaks*. It opened during an air raid and lasted only six weeks.

He was the first member of his family ever to appear on a stage.

Hates the accepted style of fashions for men. Wearing trousers, collar and tie annoys him. He is happiest when in the country. Then he wears short pants, no socks, no tie, sandals and a beret.

Is not an impromptu person. He must think about a thing before he does or says it.

Has a great intuitive sense about plays. When allowed to make his own selection he has always picked a hit.

His passion is languages. He would like to learn every language. He speaks English, French, German and American.

Only knew his wife, Ruth Martin, three weeks before they were married. They eloped. He was a soldier at the time. He was given an hour's leave of absence. Two scrubwomen in the church were the witnesses. After the ceremony he went back to the war.

Has two children. One a boy, Ronald, age eleven. The other a girl, Leslie, age five. Ronald is in school in London. Leslie is here with him.

The only sports that interest him are the three in which he indulges. He is fond of horseback riding, playing tennis and swimming in warm water.

Made his American début in 1920 in *Just Suppose*. After that he had the ill-fortune to appear in a number of failures. Speaking of that dreadful period a person recently said to Mrs. Howard: "Every first night I went to I saw your husband."

Wears a guard ring on the pinkie of his right hand. It has never been off that finger since it was given to him by his mother when he was sixteen.

He has two sisters, Irene and Doris. Has two

brothers, Arthur and Jimmy. He hasn't seen Jimmy, who is now somewhere in the wilds of Africa, for the last ten years.

His ambition is to be an author. He wrote one play, *Murray Hill*, and articles that have appeared in the *New Yorker* and *Vanity Fair*. He doesn't like acting.

Autumn shades are his favorites. Every tie he owns is brown or red. Every suit is a gray flannel or a brown tweed. When he buys a new suit it looks exactly like the one he has discarded.

At the age of sixteen he pulled a Noel Coward by writing the book, music and lyrics of a play called *Mazie's Diplomacy*. He plays piano by ear.

Two years ago his wife was very ill and underwent a serious operation. When she recovered he presented her with a Victoria Cross, which he bought in a pawnshop. "For Valor" was inscribed on it. It is her proudest possession.

He never drinks coffee but has buttermilk with every meal.

Is very keen about good music. He likes to hear a good symphony concert, but seldom attends the opera. He doesn't think the human voice can do justice to music.

His daughter says she is going to be an actress. His son dislikes the theater and has never seen him act.

He draws well. A year ago he attended an art

school with Alfred Lunt. One day they had to draw from life. The model was late. Suddenly she appeared—nude. He was so embarrassed that he couldn't look at her. When the instructor looked at Howard's drawing board he found only a mess of lines.

His hobby is photography. Has four expensive cameras and a motion picture camera. He has a pictorial record of every place he ever visited.

The greatest book ever written, he considers, is Somerset Maugham's *Of Human Bondage*. The finest of all plays, *Richard III*. His one theatrical desire is to play Richard.

Always wears a chain around his neck from which dangles an English coin. It was sent to him by his wife. He received it the opening night of *Her Cardboard Lover*. That evening the gallery stood and cheered him, an unusual occurrence in the American theater. It's been his luck charm ever since.

HE's the sole owner, publisher and editor of the bible of show business: SIME SILVERMAN.

Variety, the man in type form, is one of the best, most respected and most influential trade journal in the world.

He was fired from the Morning *Telegraph* because his review of a vaudeville act displeased the managing editor. While on that sheet he signed his reviews: "The Man in the Third Row."

He is not moody.

He is fifty-three years old. Was born in Cortland, N. Y. Has been married to the same wife for thirty years. The pride and joy of his life is his son, Syd, who wrote on *Variety* as a child critic at the age of seven, signing his articles with the pen name "Shigie."

Decided to publish a paper for the profession which would print news items and show reviews as the staff writers wrote them. He discussed the possibilities with Mrs. Silverman. Together they named it *Variety.* Then, absentmindedly, she sketched on the table cover the funny capital "V." It's still the trade-mark of the paper.

His first office was a tiny room on the fifth floor of the Knickerbocker Theatre building.

His only pet is an Angora cat named Steve.

He summers at Alexandria Bay—when he summers.

In mid-December, the year 1905, the first copy of *Variety* appeared on the newsstands. It contained sixteen pages. It sold for a nickel.

The wise guys gave the paper three months to live.

He likes to eat in road houses. His credit is good everywhere. He always pays cash.

In the beginning *Variety*'s space was devoted solely to vaudeville. Today vaudeville receives but little attention, motion pictures being the big feature.

He still reviews the small-time vaudeville shows.

Is probably the hardest working editor in America. His day begins at eight-thirty A. M. Can generally be found at his desk at two A. M. still working.

He eats in the hunting room at the Astor. Is the greatest check grabber Broadway has ever known. Has never been known to allow anyone to pick up the "bad news." Is a very liberal tipper.

He can go to bed at six in the morning and be waiting for breakfast at seven-thirty.

The thing he hates most in this world is a deadbeat.

At one time things were very bad. Most of his

staff had disappeared. He walked into the office one day to find only two men there. One was Johnny O'Connor, one of his reporters. The other was a sheriff, placed there by a creditor. They were playing rummy. It looked as if it would be necessary to get the next issue out in mimeograph form.

Variety was originally published on a Saturday. Then it moved back to Friday. Then to Thursday. Now it appears on Wednesday. This is the only respect in which it has gone backward.

He smokes Turkish cigarettes and Havana cigars. Never takes more than a dozen puffs from either. Never smokes a gift cigar. Never refuses one. His desk is always littered with expensive weeds. As his staff arrives they disappear.

His first office was so small that when one asked a question it was necessary to go into the hall to answer it. Later his office was quartered on the site where Loew's State Theatre now stands. Today he occupies an entire building in Forty-sixth Street, east of Broadway, that formerly housed Frances, the modiste. His desk is on a platform where models used to pose. It's his throne.

He weighs about 180. Has never been known to walk fast or eat slowly.

He never wears a vest.

No one but himself knows the circulation of *Variety*, and he won't tell.

He works in his shirt-sleeves. If the weather is hot he works in his undershirt.

He has little use for sports. Seldom sees a ball game, and never plays the races. His passion is auto riding. He maintains three or four high-powered cars.

A ride in the country at three in the morning is quite the usual thing for him. Generally alone or with a member of his staff.

He never carried a cane. Hates to wear the "soup and fish." Generally passes up affairs requiring this.

He dictates his business mail once weekly. The day his paper comes out. He typewrites replies to all his personal mail himself.

No one ever owned a share of stock in *Variety*. He owns it all.

Leo Carrillo was a cartoonist on *Variety*. He received a fine offer from Albee to become a vaudeville monologuist. This was one way of putting an end to his drawings.

He loves to play poker. Will sit up all night going direct to his desk from the card table. His favorite haunt is the Friars Club.

The circulation of *Variety* was built on a bicycle. He sent Johnny O'Connor on the road as circulation man. Johnny was gone fourteen months, touring the entire country and part of Canada. He hired a bicycle in each town. Made the rounds, placing *Variety* on every newsstand. Also appointed a correspondent wherever he went. In return for weekly news O'Connor gave them a credential card calling for free entry to all amusement places.

He walks with a pronounced slouch. Generally has one hand in a trousers pocket.

He maintains a private charity list. No one knows anything about it but himself and his secretary.

Was badly injured in an auto accident several years ago. Despite a few broken bones, some wrenched ligaments and what promised to be a fractured skull, he hailed a flivver and was driven forty miles to his home without asking for aid.

Variety was once advertised as "The Green Sheet." Then it carried a green cover. Then it sold for a dime. During the war the green stock became scarce and it went back to a white cover. On special editions, however, the green cover is called back into service.

His favorite drink is a Scotch highball in a tall glass.

Twenty years ago the front page of *Variety* was sold to Joe Cook for $25. Ten years ago it was sold to Irene Franklin for $2,500. Today it's news.

He has never been abroad. His paper was ten years old before he left New York to visit an outlying office. Then he went to Chicago and returned the same day he arrived.

He once had a Jap butler. But only once and not for long.

He makes notes on small pads with a tiny pencil.

He takes an ordinary lead pencil and cuts it into a number of small ones.

He is a deep thinker. Likes to cut up paper into small bits when exercising his mind. Also twirls his forelock between his thumb and forefinger. Also likes to spin his signet ring, the only jewelry he wears.

Has never been seriously ill. His sole trouble being with a trick set of teeth.

He lives on upper Central Park West. In the same building in which the late E. F. Albee lived. Occasionally they would meet in the elevator. They would never chat.

His favorite expression is "Aw, nuts."

He is the best known man on Broadway. They call him a "Square Shooter." That's Broadway's definition of all that can be expected of one of its own.

WHEN you're naming the most important playwrights of this country you've got to include GEORGE KELLY.

He has no gambling instinct whatsoever.

The tragedy of his life is winter.

He was born in Philadelphia, one of ten children. One of his brothers is Walter Kelly, famous in vaudeville as "The Virginia Judge." Another is John Kelly, who won the single sculls Olympic championship in 1920. He was privately educated and attended schools abroad. He was a weak child.

Appointments make him nervous. He worries about them in advance.

He regards the victrola and radio as fine achievements but otherwise they annoy him.

Started his theatrical career as an actor. Appeared as a headliner in vaudeville in Paul Armstrong's playlet, *The Woman Proposes*. Later took to writing his own playlets. One of these, *Poor Aubrey*, later developed into *The Show-Off*.

Rarely reads a current novel. Of all the novelists he considers Joseph Conrad the finest.

Insists upon directing his plays. Enacts every

rôle. Pays special attention to the tempo and rhythm of the play. He always says to the cast: "Let it breathe."

Eats very little meat. Doesn't drink except sauterne at meal time.

Goes out very little and often stays in his apartment for days. He is never lonely when he is alone.

When writing the room must be in perfect order. A piece of paper on the floor is enough to disturb him. He uses a typewriter and often works for eighteen hours at a stretch. Never does any rewriting, only editing.

Likes to travel. He has been everywhere from the tip of the boot of Italy to the most northern town in Norway. Avoids journeying by train whenever possible, preferring to travel by boat.

His middle name is Edward.

The only jewelry he wears is a watch (he has a drawer full of them), a necktie pin which cost a dollar and a green ring on the little finger of his right hand.

His first play was *The Torchbearers*. Since then he has written *The Show-Off, Craig's Wife* (this won the Pulitzer prize in 1925), *Daisy Mayme, Behold the Bridegroom* and *Maggie, the Magnificent* in the order named. Of these his favorite is *Behold the Bridegroom*.

When it comes to horseback riding or playing bridge, tennis and golf he is an expert.

Honestly dislikes publicity and actually goes out of his way to avoid it.

He seldom attends the theater, going about once a year. Has never seen one of his plays from the orchestra. He watches them standing in the wings.

The most amazing thing in life, he finds, is the flight of time.

Stories about wild animals interest him greatly and he reads almost every word that is written about them.

Dislikes cities. But of all the cities he has visited he likes New York the best.

He can't get too gay or he's all in.

Has no sense of direction. When he emerges from the subway the way to walk always puzzles him.

He toys at the piano and attends the opera frequently. His favorite composer is Wagner.

Hates museums. Thinks all zoos should be abolished, and would find Central Park a nice place for a stroll if it wasn't for the smell of gasoline.

He wears rest glasses when doing intensive work.

Continually amuses his friends with stories. His Southern, colored, Italian and Irish dialects are wonderful.

Has a great weakness for gents' furnishings. Is always buying them. If he lived to be a hundred years old he couldn't wear out all the things he has.

He has never seen a prize fight, a baseball game or a football game.

Has a remarkable memory. He quotes from the Bible, recites poetry by the yard and knows every line of all his plays by heart. Once he jumped into the leading rôle of *Behold the Bridegroom* with only five minutes' notice.

Before he took to the theater he was an expert draftsman. Many of the bridges now standing in Chile weren't erected until the plans were marked: "O. K. George Kelly."

He calls this "The Vulgar Age." An age in which manners are at their lowest ebb.

ARTHUR HOPKINS. The sphinx of the show business.

He scares people by saying nothing.

Was born October 4, 1878. His father was a doctor. He has seven brothers. All, with the exception of one, are professional men. The one, William Rowland Hopkins, is at present City Manager of Cleveland. This corresponds to the title of Mayor here.

Is a conservative dresser. Generally wears a derby or a gray felt hat. He always wears a bow tie.

He was the first director in America to permit an actor to talk with his back to the audience.

Was once a reporter. Is noted for invading the Polish district of Cleveland and capturing the only photograph of Czolgosz, the assassinator of President McKinley. Every newspaper used this photograph, giving due credit.

He is the author of the book, *How's Your Second Act?*

Loves to play golf. Two of his best friends are Sam H. Harris and Arthur Hammerstein. They are known as "the Three Golfing H's."

His office is a cubicle room in the Plymouth

Theatre. He sits in his chair there, saddle fashion. His desk is piled high with manuscripts. Occasionally he gets reading jags and does nothing for days but read plays.

He is stubborn.

When he first started producing his efforts were rapped by the critics. He said: "I will be producing plays when all those boys are gone and forgotten." The critics of that day were DeFoe, Reamer, Dale, Davies and Wolf. They are all gone. Years later the same Mr. Hopkins wrote: "I want no praise for bad work. If they find me careless or gross, cheap or vulgar, my head is on the block for them."

His middle name is Melancthon.

Whenever he discovers what he thinks is an "author" he goes nuts.

Lives in Great Neck. Among his prize possessions there are a baby grand piano, a victrola, his wife—Eva McDonald—and a handsome mahogany poker outfit.

He bought *On Trial* by giving Elmer Rice a $50 advance. Then produced the play under the Cohan and Harris banner by giving them a fifty per cent interest in the play. During one of the rehearsals he thought of the revolving stage. This made it possible to do the now famous flashback in twenty-six seconds.

Gets a big kick out of doing things people don't expect him to do.

Is more agreeable when he has a flop than when he has a hit.

He never wears jewelry.

When rehearsing a play the stage curtain is always down. He sits in a chair or stands in the wings, smoking. Sometimes it is days before he says a word. For at least seven days the cast merely sit and read their parts. When he thinks that they understand the play thoroughly, he allows them to act. He never tells an actor what to do, but what not to do.

He tells the truth or nothing at all.

Has a terrific admiration for Robert Edmond Jones, Isadora Duncan and Raquel Meller.

Is the only producer who quotes himself in advertisements.

When he produced *What Price Glory* he thought real soldiers could play soldiers better than actors. Every soldier in that play, with the exception of the principals, had done service abroad.

His great passion is discovering new talent.

Has the ability actually to forget things he doesn't wish to remember.

He writes most of the statements that are issued by the Producing Managers Association.

Every Christmas he tries to be in Cleveland for a reunion dinner with his brothers.

On the opening night of a play he does one of two things. He either sits in the light gallery, which hangs over the first balcony, and watches the play and the audience or he sits backstage, near the stage door, with his back to the players, listening to the lines and the applause.

His favorite haunt is the Lotus Club.

Once one of his brothers visited him at the office. It is said that both sat there for half an hour before either greeted the other.

He keeps a cow on his estate at Great Neck because he insists on fresh milk every morning.

He knows more than he will talk about. Therefore, is given credit for knowing much more than he says.

The rest is silence.

THE GHETTO GIRL

MOLLY PICON. The darling of East Broadway.

She is not quite five feet and weighs a hundred pounds. Wears a size eleven girl's dress. Her toes never reach the tip of her stockings.

She is always asking questions.

Her one disappointment in life is that she wasn't born a boy.

Made her stage début as an infant prodigy at amateur nights. In those days she was "Baby Margaret." Ten years ago in Boston she deserted vaudeville for the Yiddish stage by joining a Jewish burlesque show. She speaks English better than many actors on Broadway.

Has a mania for French dolls. Her apartment is cluttered with them.

She writes the lyrics of all her songs. For every show she learns something new. She can sing, dance, perform feats of magic, play six different musical instruments and do acrobatic tricks.

Hates to talk on the telephone. If she is home alone she never answers the phone but lets it keep on ringing.

In every play she wears a dress suit. She owns one dress suit with three pairs of pants.

Always sits with her feet on the chair.

She is married. When she first met her husband, Jacob Kalish, he never combed his hair, shined his shoes or pressed his trousers. She told him that if he dolled up she'd marry him. He immediately bought three suits and invited her to his house. He then changed suits every half hour. There was nothing left for her to do but marry him. She proudly states that he can make love to her in six different languages.

She carries Jewish luck charms given to her by rabbis.

Whenever she has a new dress she goes to the Royal Café. This is the Reuben's, Sardi's and Algonquin of Second Avenue.

Is always putting her fingers in her mouth but never bites her nails.

When it comes to naming a favorite actor and actress, Charlie Chaplin and Helen Hayes head her honor roll.

She has performed in Russia, Roumania, Galicia, Jerusalem and Austria. The results of this tour were a gift from Queen Marie of Roumania, the finding of Joseph Rumshinsky (he now writes the music for all her plays) in Vienna and the naming of two gardens after her in Jerusalem.

During intermission she always drinks a glass of tea with lemon.

Offstage she never uses powder, lipstick or perfume. She doesn't smoke.

She wears both nightgowns and pajamas. She buys neither. It is the custom of the Yiddish theater to have a "Testimonial Evening" once a month. On these occasions she receives nightgowns and pajamas from admirers.

When she was born the midwife looked at her and said: "Nebesh—poor kid." Her mother didn't kiss her until she was a year old.

Is actually afraid of people who talk figures. Has no head for business. Her husband arranges all her financial affairs.

She gets a big kick out of reading poetry and visiting the Metropolitan Museum of Art. Her favorite author is Ben Hecht. In her opinion *One Thousand and One Afternoons in Chicago* is one of the finest books ever written.

D. W. Griffith is her most ardent admirer. He intends to star her shortly in a talking picture.

She lives with her husband, mother and sister. Her husband is a part owner of Kessler's Second Avenue Theatre, where she performs. Her mother is a wardrobe mistress at that theater. Her sister does the cooking for the family. They keep a kosher house. Outside, however, Molly loves to go to a Chinese restaurant and eat roast pork.

On the East Side they name kids and clubs after her.

Once every year on a certain Jewish holiday she plays for the prisoners at Sing Sing.

During her entire career she received only one mash note. And that was from a college boy who had to write it as part of his initiation to join a fraternity.

Continually suffers from tonsillitis. In fact she was brought up on it.

When she was four years old she had only thirteen hairs on her head. Her nickname was "Chayve rive mit di dtraitzen haar." Which in plain English means: "Molly with the thirteen hairs."

She keeps a book at home in which she makes every prominent visitor write his name.

She went to Niagara Falls for her honeymoon. On the homeward trip, the happy couple were robbed of their baggage, their money, in fact everything. They arrived at Molly's mother's house in a taxi and had to borrow money from her to pay the fare. The mother put her arms around Molly and with tears in her eyes said: "My poor daughter. She goes on a honeymoon and she loses everything." To which Molly quickly replied: "But I had a good time."

She is very nervous on opening nights. On two occasions she lost her voice completely while on the stage.

Every day her husband gives her a list of "Don'ts."

RING LARDNER. He came to New York to do nothing and has been a failure ever since. Was born in Niles, Mich. The great event took place forty-six years ago. Always looks seven years younger than he really is.

He bites his tongue while writing.

Elmer the Great was his first play. While it was current he made his friends call him "Fanny."

In the way of drinks his taste runs to any glass that is filled with anything but champagne. Champagne makes him nauseous.

As a newspaper man he worked in crowded offices with people talking and writing all around him. Today he can't even begin to work if there is anybody else in the room.

He has never murdered anybody. If he does you can lay two to one that the party will be the author of a poem, story or play that is the least bit whimsical.

Occasionally he spends an entire day in a restaurant.

Was once paid five hundred dollars by a pottery concern to make a speech at their annual convention.

His first magazine story was about ball players. He sent it to the *Saturday Evening Post*. Not only did they buy the story but they encouraged him to write the now famous "You Know Me Al" yarns.

He'd rather be alone than with anybody excepting four or five people. He believes this is mutual.

Was among those who were the guests of Albert D. Lasker on the *Leviathan*'s trial trip. While he was on the boat he never saw the ocean.

Whenever he wants to laugh he goes to see Will Rogers, Ed Wynn, W. C. Fields, Jack Donahue, Harry Watson and Beatrice Lillie. If it is acting that he desires to see he hurries to a play with Alfred Lunt, Walter Huston, Lynn Fontanne or Helen Hayes. Otherwise he attends the opera.

He has flat feet.

Doesn't care for parties. Unless he is giving them. Because then he can order as often as he likes.

Was fired from the Boston *American* in 1911. Went back to Chicago, his favorite shooting gallery, and asked the Chicago *American* for a job. The managing editor inquired: "What was the matter in Boston?" He replied: "Oh, nothing; except that I was fired." The managing editor said: "That's the best recommendation you could have. Go to work."

Is the author of the following books: *The Love Nest, What of It? How to Write Short Stories, Gullible's Travels, The Big Town* and a modest autobiography titled: *The Story of a Wonder Man.*

He can play the piano, the saxophone, the clarinet and the cornet. But not so good.

Has what is called "perfect pitch." That is, he can tell which key anyone is singing or playing in without looking or asking. Once won $2 at this stunt. It really isn't an accomplishment he can live on.

He is a passionate collector of passport pictures and license photographs of taxi drivers.

Among the things that annoy him are writing letters, answering the telephone, signing checks, attending banquets, untying the knot in his shoe-lace, filling his fountain pen and trying to find handkerchiefs to match his neckwear.

Before he dies he hopes to write a successful novel. Believes he is going to live to a ripe old age.

Begins his stories with just a character in mind. Hardly ever knows what the plot is going to be until two-thirds through with the story.

He dislikes work (except the writing of lyrics), scenes like the Victor Herbert thing in the 1928 *Scandals,* insomnia, derby hats, beauty marks, motion pictures (excepting those Chaplin is in), dirty stories and adverse criticism—whether fair or not.

The W is for Wilmer.

He was standing at a bar in New Orleans during Mardi Gras time three years ago and a Southern gentleman tried to entertain him by telling how old and Southern and aristocratic his family was. Lardner interrupted the Southerner after twenty minutes of it with the remark that he was born in Michigan of colored parentage.

Recently he offered a cigarette concern this advertising slogan: "Not a Cigarette in a Carload." They didn't accept it.

He is noted for sending funny telegrams. One of the most famous is the one he sent when he was unable to attend a dinner. It read: "Sorry cannot be with you tonight, but it is the children's night out and I must stay home with the maid."

MAMMY!!! AL JOLSON. He drinks a bucket of bromo-seltzer every day.

Is very superstitious. He is always knocking wood.

His real name is Asa Yoelson. Got the name Jolson when he was the singing mascot for a regiment in the Spanish-American war. A soldier asked him what his name was. He replied "Yoelson." The soldier said: "That's a Swedish name—you're no Swede. Your name's Jolson only you don't know how to pronounce it." From then on Jolson was his name.

Although he has been married three times women play a small part in his life.

He owns part of the St. Louis National Baseball Club.

His first appearance at the Winter Garden was in the show that opened that theater, *Little Miss Innocence*. It would be great to record that he made a big hit. The truth of the matter is that he made his first appearance on the stage after midnight and that no one paid any attention to him.

Likes to be patted on the back and is always surrounded by "Yes-men." It was Walter Winchell who asked: "How many yes-men make a Jolson?"

Is not on speaking terms with his brother Harry. He wishes his brother wouldn't use his name.

He has to read something in order to fall asleep.

Once started work in a D. W. Griffith picture. Then went to court in order to break the contract. On the witness stand he said: "I knew I was terrible and would never make a hit in pictures." He was released from the contract. Today he has revolutionized the motion picture industry.

He cracks his knuckles when he is nervous.

His big passion in life is applause. Let an audience encourage him and he'll break a vocal cord.

As a kid he sang on the streets of Washington and in the backroom of saloons. His boyhood pal at that time was Bill Robinson.

He is known as the best second verse writer in Tin Pan Alley. He doesn't keep the profits on his songs but donates them to a tuberculosis camp.

Hates cold weather. So much so that one frosty night in Chicago he returned to his hotel room after the evening's performance of *Bombo*. While undressing he noticed a sign across the street blinking: "It's June in Miami. It's June in Miami." The next morning he was on his way to Miami, leaving the show cold.

He beams with happiness if anyone compliments him on his ballroom dancing.

Never took a singing lesson until he was past

thirty-five. Then stopped after the sixth lesson because he thought they were hurting his voice.

He's as sentimental as his songs.

Is a great showman and never misses an opportunity. When he arrived in Hollywood to make *The Jazz Singer* the entire town was at the station to meet him. He sang: "California, Here I Come."

Mark Hellinger is now writing his life story. Hellinger got all his data when he accompanied the singing fool on his honeymoon abroad. Mark was the odd man.

His favorite word is "baby."

He bet as much as $100,000 on a horse race and lost.

Never laughs at a joke except to be polite. If the joke really amuses him he says with a serious face, "That's very funny."

He knows a kosher restaurant in almost every important town.

Was a personal friend of Presidents Woodrow Wilson and Warren G. Harding. One evening he had dinner with President Harding at the White House. Pork chops was the dish and every time he picked one up the President's dog, Laddie Boy, would jump and grab it. This wouldn't have happened if Jolson had been using his knife and fork.

He likes to drive a car fast.

If he ever has a son he wants him to be like Buddy De Sylva.

His favorite game is Hearts. If he loses he makes alibis. If he wins he gloats over the victory.

Although he refused $20,000 to play the Roxy for one week, he sang songs for nothing merely to help his wife, Ruby Keeler.

Although a sure-fire performer he suffers more from stage fright than the rankest amateur. Eight o'clock one evening on the opening of a Winter Garden show he was found wandering bareheaded in the rain on Fifth Avenue and had to be taken to the theater.

He is really one of the loneliest guys in the world.

His father was not a cantor. He was a "schochet." This is a man who kills chickens and makes them kosher.

When Ruby Keeler opened in *Whoopee* in Pittsburgh he sent this telegram to Eddie Cantor: "Remember, this is the first time a Cantor was ever billed over a Jolson."

He is good-natured. But on occasion he displays a furious temper. When in this state he has a pretty good right hook.

If he could figure out a way to be in two places at the same time, he'd be happy.

When he married Ruby Keeler he had two wedding rings with him because he wasn't certain of the size of her finger.

He will not sleep in a hotel room one of whose windows opens on a fire escape. He will not sleep in any room alone. One night when he had to do so he piled all the furniture in the room against the door.

He has spies for gags. If he's in Hollywood and a nifty is cracked on Broadway it is wired to him.

He is stage-struck.

Mae West. She was born in Brooklyn, August 17, 1900, according to her life insurance policy and the record on the police blotter at Blackwell's Island. Several acquaintances claim to have known her before that date.

She uses a floral perfume in the morning. In the evening she changes to a heavy Oriental perfume.

Years ago she played the Palace in "Songs, Dances and Witty Sayings." She is the originator of the shimmy. Discarded it before Gilda Gray and Bee Palmer took up the sway.

All her leading men have been six footers. She prefers the "he-man" type.

Doesn't smoke. The cigarettes she smokes on the stage are denicotinized.

Her conversation bubbles with slang. Will often invent certain phrases and expressions all her own. Also will render an original pronunciation of a word. When talking she covers a world of territory by continually saying: "Know what I mean."

Her ears are really beautiful.

She has a brother and a sister. Her father was a prize fighter. Later a bouncer at Fox's Folly Theater.

Besides English, she speaks German, French and Jewish.

Her first big rôle was with Ed Wynn in *Sometime*. Later she appeared in Ziegfeld and Shubert revues. In one of these she was Cleopatra and shimmied in a number called "Shakespeare's Garden of Love."

She always wears a pendant in the shape of a champagne bottle.

She has the same mannerisms offstage as on. When acting, however, her voice is three times lower than usual.

In writing a play she needs only an idea. After making a few rough notes she calls a rehearsal. A script is not essential. She writes the dialogue and works out the situations during rehearsals to fit the cast she has hired. Will often ask the actors if they like a certain line. If they don't she will change it. Reading a part, she believes, makes an actor self-conscious. Before she wrote plays for herself she learned her rôles by having them read to her.

As a kid she was dressed in Little Lord Fauntleroy clothing.

Her favorite dish is kippered herring.

She likes everything massive. Her furniture, bed, even her car is larger than the average. The swan bed used in *Diamond Lil* was taken from her home. Formerly it belonged to Diamond Jim Brady.

She has never tried to reduce.

Seldom reads. When a public event like the Ruth Snyder case interests her she has it read to her. When she does read, it is an ancient history book.

Is of the opinion that *Sex* will become a classic. That in time it will be revived like *Ghosts* or *Hamlet*.

She sleeps in a black lace nightgown. Lying flat on her back with her right arm over her eyes.

Some day she hopes to own a leopard for a pet.

Her ambition is to write a Pulitzer Prize Play.

She receives at least four proposals of marriage a week. And from some of the town's best blue blood.

When dressing she first puts on her shoes and stockings. Then combs her hair and puts on her hat. Then she puts on her dress. All her dresses are made to order with special slits to enable her to do this. They are all cut very low about the neck.

In vaudeville she also worked in an acrobatic act. She can lift a 500-pound weight. She can support three men each weighing 150 pounds.

She kisses on the stage with all the fervor that she does off. During an intense love scene in the play her pulse will jump twenty-eight beats.

Her pet aversion is a man who wears white socks.

She has a colored maid who is a dead ringer for her. She will color her own photograph to show a visitor the likeness.

She believes virtue always triumphs over vice.

In a business where an ironclad contract often becomes merely a scrap of paper, there is a man whose word is his bond. He often closes an important deal by merely a handshake. The man is Sam H. Harris.

The "H" is for Henry, although he likes to believe it stands for "Hits."

His first theatrical job was at Miner's Theater. Was employed to trail John W. Kelly, the Rolling Mill Man, a star of the times. When Kelly went out for a drink he played no favorites. He gave every saloon along the Bowery a break. Harris's task was to tag after him and bring him back to the theater in time to go on.

When a young girl comes to him, anxious to get into show business, he advises her to go home and get married.

At twenty-two he owned six horses. Entered four of them in a seven-horse race. They finished fourth, fifth, sixth and seventh. He immediately traded his stable of horses for a bulldog.

His favorite expression is: "You can play only one way—straight."

Was once part of one of the most successful partnerships in the theatrical business: Cohan and Harris. That firm dissolved, friendly, during the actors' strike. Cohan picked up a blotter, which had his picture in one corner and Harris's in another. Tearing the blotter, he tossed the half with Harris's picture to him and said: "Sam, we're through." That's all there was to it.

His trousers can stay up without support of either a belt or suspenders.

Always sits in the last row of the balcony at the opening of his plays.

Is the only theatrical producer to have the honor of having a book dedicated to him by Alexander Woollcott.

He hasn't a gray hair in his head. Bets have actually been made that he never will have a gray hair.

His idea of a swell meal is a good bowl of vegetable soup.

Any play he produces must have these two requisites: In his own words, "It must add up at the finish." Secondly, it must contain at least one character for whom the audience will root.

He never harbors a grudge.

Was once in the prize-fighting racket. Trained his protégé faithfully. Only to see him knocked out in the first five minutes of action. While this man was being counted out, he was in the other corner, signing up the winner. You've probably heard of the guy—Terry McGovern.

He eats chop suey only on rainy days.

In his opinion there is no man in the world who knows the theater as well as George M. Cohan.

Every time he is about to close a show, his comment is: "I can't go along with it."

Is now the owner of a fine stable of horses. He names his horses after fond memories. One is called Terry McGovern. Another is known as Sadie Thompson.

As a kid he greatly admired John Drew. Although just getting out of short pants he grew a heavy mustache in order to look like his idol.

His favorite author is George S. Kaufman. And, as far as music is concerned, his taste begins and ends with Irving Berlin.

He once worked in a hat store on Grand Street. Every week he had to make a delivery away uptown, at Seventy-second Street. For this he was given a quarter for carfare. He walked, thus giving a dollar a month extra to his mother. Every month his mother had to buy him a pair of shoes costing a dollar and a quarter. A little figuring and shortly he was told to spend the quarter for carfare. His economy was costing the family money.

He will play cards with anybody in the world but Harpo Marx.

199

His office is a studio room in the Music Box Theatre. A wall door leads to an especially constructed dungeon. Inside there is a fully equipped bar. The entrance is guarded by a cuckoo clock. While leaning against the bar the pressing of a button will produce a beautiful scenic effect. The ceiling becomes "Blue Heaven" and the stars twinkle.

When an actress's performance pleases him he expresses his delight by saying: "She gives me a lump."

KELCEY ALLEN. He's the dramatic critic of *Women's Wear*, a he-man's newspaper.

He was on Broadway when Jed Harris was a spindle-legged kid taking violin lessons in Newark. When Shanley's was situated at the crossroads of the world and didn't know it. When George White ran away from home to become a jockey. When the mob gathered at the Metropole bar. When Earl Carroll, a big boy for his age, walked the streets of Pittsburgh in a white sailor suit and "Throw 'Em Down McCloskey" was the popular tune of the day. Today he's godmother to New York's dramatic critics.

He talks with authority on any subject.

His first name is Eugene. But he doesn't use it because he is a believer in numerology.

Started his theatrical career by carrying copy for the critics. In those yesteryears the critics wrote their reviews in the theater. He called for their copy, delivering it to their respective papers. He received twenty-five cents from each critic. He looked mighty cute riding about town on a bicycle.

Is happily married to a most charming lady.

He types with two fingers. And generally stubs them.

He is the best broadcasting station this side of the Rocky Mountains.

He lives at the Hotel Chelsea but gets his mail at the Hermitage Hotel.

Writes his reviews on the second floor of the Fitzgerald Building. It takes him an hour and a half to do so. Then takes the review home, places it under his pillow and sleeps on it. A messenger calls for his copy every morning at nine.

He suffers from new diseases only.

Has attended more than 5,000 first nights.

Knows more about Broadway than any man in the Garment Center. Knows more about the Garment Center than any man on Broadway.

His father was a school teacher. Had a degree in philology. Spoke nine languages.

He knows every restaurant in town that serves an eighty-cent table d'hôte dinner. Also knows their daily specials without looking at the menu.

Has a repertoire of stories. Tells them again and again. Employing the same gestures.

He's the best audience he ever had.

Visited Europe last summer and was received by the Pope. His trip was ruined, however, on hearing that a producer had withdrawn his advertisement from *Women's Wear*.

He notices legs but can't carry a tune.

Carries a folding wallet which when spread out would cover the dance floor of a night club. It contains passes for everything in town, from the Aquarium to the Metropolitan Opera House. Also carries patent medicines with him. No matter what ails you he's got something that will cure you.

Tells things in detail. Then says: "Now what I mean to say is this—" And he starts all over again.

Smokes cigars and only offers them to people who don't smoke.

Actually placed himself on every opening-night list. He published a sheet listing all the critics. Mailed it to the press agents for their convenience. He placed his name on the list. Before long he was complaining about the location of his seats.

He perspires freely about the neck. When attending a banquet (his favorite indoor and outdoor sport) he always carries an extra collar with him.

Calls people by their wrong names. When corrected says: "I know it's his wrong name, but I call him that."

In Sardi's he once made a flip crack about an Italian who had a mustache which extended fully six inches on both sides. The playboys of the Rialto got busy. They told Kelcey the man had overheard him and threatened him. For two days he stayed away—frightened. On his return he immediately sought out the man with the mustache and said:

"That remark you overheard wasn't about you. I'm sorry if you think so and I want to apologize." The Italian rose, stared at Kelcey and said: "Me no spik English."

His hobby is collecting newspapers with typographical errors.

He carries a watch which would be a burden for a Singer midget. Instead of the customary numerals there are Hebraic letters.

He can and does eat anything. His favorite dish, however, is knackwurst completely buried in sauerkraut.

The thing he cherishes most is his name plate in the Chanin Theatre. When first nighting there he polishes it with his sleeve.

He dines daily at every table in Sardi's.

Whenever anybody becomes angry with him, he buys that person a present with the hope of becoming friendly again.

He wobbles when he walks.

His monthly telephone bill is very low. He seldom calls anybody. Whenever he wishes to speak to someone on the phone he sends the party a postal card asking that person to call him.

He never walks out on a show no matter how bad it is. However, one evening he was seen leaving the theater before the end of the musical comedy. The producer of that show called him up the next day to learn why. Luckily, Kelcey wasn't home. But his wife was. After listening to the manager's complaint about Kelcey's walking out, Mrs. Allen said: "I'm so sorry and I do hope you'll forgive him. You see, Kelcey walks in his sleep."

He memorizes obituaries. He would like nothing better than to be able to read his own.

ONCE upon a time there were four Hawaiians. And this guy got famous because he wouldn't imitate them. JOE COOK.

His real name was Joseph Lopez. Was orphaned at the age of four. Then adopted by a family named Cook in Evansville, Ind. He spent his teens in a cold water flat on Amsterdam Avenue near 135th Street.

He is extremely superstitious. He knocks wood. Will not walk under a ladder for all the money in the world.

Talks exactly the same offstage as he does on. With a slow drawl.

When a youngster in Evansville he organized a kid show. The theater was the family barn. He charged five cents for admission and actually made money. At fifteen he was playing on the Keith circuit with his brother Leo.

He always wears a cap. Wears a hat on the street very seldom. On each occasion he felt as conspicuous as a kid in his first long pants. He wears suspenders, unshined shoes and $200 suits.

Can often be found in a shooting gallery pecking away at the clay pipes.

Dave Chasen can't do the funny hand business used in *Rain or Shine* without him.

He lives at Lake Hopatcong. Drives home every night after his performance if he's playing in town.

Made his début in show business as grip carrier for the Great Doctor Dunham. Before the doctor gave his spiel on the magic medicine which cured corns, colds and ingrown nails, he did a juggling act. He finished the season stranded in a tank town. He was paid off in medicine bottles.

He has worn out forty-one pairs of roller skates. Seventeen bicycles. Two motor-cycles. Eight automobiles and four motor boats.

His first vaudeville salary was $50 a week. His latest was $2,750.

They're still looking for four Hawaiians who can imitate him.

He is one of the most versatile performers in America. Here are merely a few of his feats: Plain and fancy hand juggling. Japanese foot juggling. Sharpshooting from a slack wire. Trapeze balancing. Propels a huge ball up a fifteen foot incline with his feet. Plays various musical instruments. Exhibits skill as a clog dancer. Ditto as an acrobatic dancer. Furnishes motive power for a foot propelled merry-go-round. Does various feats of magic. Catches (or misses) lighted matches with his mouth. Extracts music from an insane Ferris wheel contraption. Casually tosses a bouquet to himself with one foot.

His understudy is the Barnum & Bailey Circus.

His parents were in the show business. His father retired from the stage to become a successful portrait painter.

Has a passion for a good cook stove. Loves to cook spaghetti, chili-con-carne and mulligan stew. Has cooked for as many as three hundred people at one sitting.

He is very modest and blushes easily.

Has a piano on which he makes every guest burn his signature. The piano has 948 names on it. Including such as Ring Lardner, Gilbert Seldes, Robert Benchley, Babe Ruth, Charles MacArthur and Hudson Maxim.

He has many week-end parties at his home. Generally has from five to a dozen males but never a woman.

Dave Chasen, one of the funny fellows in his act, is his right-hand man. Dave even carries his money for him.

His major delight is discovering an odd restaurant. Is seldom seen at any prominent eating place. Will walk miles to find a hole-in-the-wall beanery where a newfangled dish is offered.

One thing he can't stand is the sissy type of man. Especially the fellow who says "Tummy" for stomach. "Hanky" for handkerchief. He thinks there should be a law.

His dressing room is plastered with signs saying: "No Smoking." "Positively No Smoking." "Absolutely No Smoking." There is one large sign which has "No Smoking" written out in twenty-six languages, including the Scandinavian. He doesn't mind if you smoke.

He is quite an artist at short-changing.

He never saw a real Hawaiian. Once saw a Hawaiian act in vaudeville. The Hula dancer was a dazzling blonde who wore a wig. One of the Hawaiians was Buddy De Sylva, the song writer.

His favorite drink is a glass of real beer. After the third stein he sings the original version of "Frankie and Johnny."

Has only one servant at his country home. This servant is the butler, the cook, the chauffeur, etc. The servant has a different name and uniform for each job.

He was the second white man to play the ukulele.

DOROTHY GISH. She is five feet four inches. Weighs a hundred five pounds. Wears a size four shoe. She has gray eyes. When she wears a blue hat, however, they appear bluish.

She has traveled from New York to Hollywood forty times.

Is the proud possessor of six first editions and an original letter from Byron, denying that he wrote "The Vampire."

The Gish girls, still in pigtails, began their theatrical careers touring the country in "10–20 and 30" melodramas in the days when movies were not only unheard of but also unseen.

Her first rôle was Little Will' in *East Lynne*. Her next appearance was with Lillian Gish in *Her First False Step*. Lillian played the rôle of Her First False Step. She was The Second False Step.

Doesn't know a thing about cards. Consequently, she doesn't play. She calls clubs, clovers.

For the last seven years she has been married to James Rennie.

Is not athletically inclined. Would much rather go shopping than play golf or tennis.

She is happiest when traveling. Will take a long trip on the slightest provocation. Many times she has left a happy home, almost on a moment's notice, to sojourn in Italy, France, England, Cuba, and Rising Sun, Ohio.

She attended school for only two years. Reads omnivorously to make up for this. Read Schopenhauer when she was fourteen.

When she appeared in New York recently everybody asked her, "How's Hollywood?" She hasn't been in Hollywood since 1919. She has been working in studios in Italy, England, France and New York.

Is terribly superstitious. The first thing she does when she arrives in a town is to look up the local fortune teller.

She has never seen a prize fight, a Bernard Shaw play, Rin-Tin-Tin, a bicycle race, a Turkish bath or Van Cortlandt Park.

Every night before retiring she washes her stockings.

Very seldom attends the movies. Has seen only six pictures during the last two years.

Has had her hair treated by the same hairdresser for the last ten years. No matter where she may travel the hairdresser goes along. When playing in a picture she will not change her hair to fit the rôle, but wears a wig.

She believes that all men should be tall, dark and handsome.

Her favorite drink is a frosted chocolate. And that tastes simply horrid to her unless she can sip it through a straw.

Made most of her big pictures abroad. *Nell Gwynn* and *Madame Pompadour* were made in England. *Romola* was made in Italy. *The Bright Shawl* in Havana.

In 1917 she was in France making *Hearts of the World*. She survived ten air raids.

When in New York she lives in Gramercy Park Place.

Once she attended a bull fight. She fainted and had to be carried out of the arena.

She has a canary named John Gish and a dog called "Nebisch." Also a parrot who can only say: "You can teach a parrot to say that it is just as good, but he won't know what he's talking about."

Fog fascinates her. For this reason she would rather live in London than any other place in the world.

She sleeps with her mouth closed.

She can remember when the Gish family, composed of herself, Lillian and their mother, had only fifteen cents to spend for luncheon. They would invest as follows: Ten cents worth of ice cream and five cents worth of ladyfingers.

As child actresses they followed the Smith family, Gladys, Lottie and Jack, in a play called *In Convict Stripes*. These three later became known as Mary, Lottie and Jack Pickford.

Her favorite dish is Crêpes Suzette, which in plain English is Jewish blintzers.

She simply adores dancing, and thought seriously of entering the dance marathon that took place at Madison Square Garden some time ago.

Her mother and sister didn't attend the opening of *Young Love* because they were too nervous and because they had heard the play was a bit naughty. But Dorothy received this wire: "No matter what you do mother and I still love you."

She has had seven "sweet sixteen" parties.

!!!***@@@!!!***

SOME day someone will write another *Royal Family*. It will be a tale of the mad, mad Bennetts. For that author, here's some data about the head of the clan: RICHARD BENNETT.

He is always positive.

Has two favorite dishes. One is plain lamb chops. The other is a bowl of wilted lettuce.

Has three daughters. Joan, Constance and Barbara. All began their careers by performing in the movies.

When he rehearsed in *Jarnegan* he wore only a pink nightgown.

Drinks a quart of Apollinaris water every day on rising. Gets the water free by mentioning it in the play he happens to be in.

He calls the box office from his dressing room before every performance to ask how the house is. Doesn't give instructions to raise the curtain until satisfied.

Likes to encourage extras. Tells them that he rose from the ranks himself. He never was an extra in his life.

Claims a man's best friend is his press agent and

his worst enemy an ex-wife. He has two of each.

Always does rewriting on plays in which he appears. *What Every Woman Knows* he believes to be the best play he ever appeared in. Because he didn't have to do any rewriting with that, he considers Sir James Barrie the greatest writer in the world.

He can talk a great fight. His right hook, however, is a thing to duck.

After *What Every Woman Knows* closed and he parted with Maude Adams, he took advantage of the fact that she was opening in *Chanticleer* to send her this wire: "I congratulate you on the realization of your fondest ambition—at last you are your own leading man."

He retires at four every morning. Rises promptly at twelve. Eats only one meal a day. That at six o'clock. However, he loves to act in plays that give him a chance to eat on the stage.

Hates interviewers who don't come armed with complete information about his career. Tells them to consult Who's Who—which contains only a fragmentary account.

Makes a curtain speech every time he has something to get off his chest. The stage is his soap box.

His luck charm is a white elephant.

If an actor stands in the wings talking while he is acting he invents some excuse to leave the stage.

Then tells the actor to stop talking or have his head knocked off.

If the front door of the theater is opened by some peerer-in he stops acting until the glare from the outside has passed. If particularly annoyed he steps to the front of the stage and yells at the person.

His favorite literature is "The Songs of Solomon."

Wants to be cremated when he dies so he'll be used to it when he gets there.

Holds a kind of soirée in his dressing room every night after the second act. Has hundreds of visitors. Mostly broken down actors, rich acquaintances and young feminine admirers.

He likes to frighten Boy Scouts.

He counts that day lost when he doesn't add a new line to the play he happens to be in.

Spends so much time in adjusting makeup that he never leaves the theater after a matinée. Thus avoids removing and replacing the grease-paint. Passes the time between performances by either sleeping or entertaining.

He plays the piano, banjo and guitar. Believes that he could make a living as a tap dancer.

His wife is his attention caller. She plays solitaire in his dressing room every evening.

He never wore a wig. Dyes his hair to suit the

rôle. His hair has been blond, black, brown, red and gray.

He insists upon owning the road rights of any show he is in. Quarreled with the Theatre Guild over *Playing at Love*, later titled *Caprice*, because of this and quit the show.

No woman with a double chin is beautiful to him.

When traveling he carries with him a necktie board that irons them while you sleep.

He is a man of much talent. Shaves himself. Manicures his own nails. Cuts his own hair.

Once at Texas Guinan's night club he drew a Bible from his hip pocket and read it to the assemblage. Everybody kept quiet and listened. He panicked them.

He wears only a green smock when sleeping.

Considers himself one of the ten greatest actors in the world. Has a difficult time naming the other nine. Generally being unable to get past Forbes-Robertson.

No matter what play he is appearing in he never promises to go on for more than one act.

He has one hair growing on each shoulder.

A. H. WOODS. His real label is Albert Herman. Without knowing a thing about numerology, he made his name initials. Then added the tag of Woods, taking it from N. S. Woods, an actor whom he worshiped.

He greets everyone, regardless of sex, with: "Hello, sweetheart."

Was a billposter. His real entry into show business was when he took a piece of lithograph paper to Theodore Kremer. Commissioned him to write a play about it. The picture was of the Bowery. Kremer had the measles at the time. The finished product was *The Bowery After Dark.*

His favorite combination of colors is yellow and black.

All his business correspondence ends with: "With Love and Kisses."

Owen Davis used to write two plays a week for him. Still considers *Bertha, the Sewing Machine Girl,* and *Nellie, the Beautiful Cloak Model,* the two best plays Davis ever wrote. Davis doesn't.

Believes any play Samuel Shipman writes in Atlantic City is worth reading.

He hired his own Boswell in the person of Samuel Hoffenstein, who now does things in praise of practically nothing. Instead of recording the actual doings Hoffenstein allowed his imagination to write the life of Woods. Thus a character was created. One which he often tries to live up to. He believes what he reads.

He sits with both feet resting on the chair.

Wore a dress suit only once in his life. It was at the opening of the Guitrys. He hired it for the occasion. Is very proud of the fact that Otto Kahn said he looked good.

He believes in luck and does most everything by hunches.

William Randolph Hearst practically produced *The Road to Ruin* for him without knowing it. Hearst gave him $500 to move out of one of his buildings. With this he started anew.

Will get up from his desk after a day's work and depart for Europe with all the thought and preparation that you give to going to a movie.

Has made numerous trips to Europe with only a toothbrush in his pocket. While on the ship he occasionally worries where he is going to get the toothpaste.

He reads six plays a day. Will often buy a play by merely hearing an outline of the plot.

Once walked into Hammerstein's Victoria Theater. Saw a pretty girl on the stage. Became quite enthused. Decided that a girl so beautiful deserved to be starred in a legitimate play. The girl was Julian Eltinge. He went through with it anyway.

Has a clay statue of a negro youth in his office for luck. In the hand of this youth he always places a copy of the script of his latest production.

Walter Moore is his best friend. For this there is a penalty. He is his companion on most of the sudden trips.

He uses the most profane language without quite realizing what it means. The rougher his language the better he likes you. When he talks pleasantly keep away.

His office is decorated with artificial flowers.

Every month he orders a thousand cigars. He chews a cigar more than he smokes it. Everybody always knows what part of the building he is in. He leaves a trail of ashes.

He knows George Bernard Shaw personally and calls him Buddy. There is no record of what Shaw calls him.

Douglas Fairbanks, Mary Pickford and Charlie Chaplin worked for him before they entered the movies. He let them go because they wanted more money. Chaplin was getting twenty-five dollars a week and asked for thirty.

His favorite eating place is his office. Every day he has vegetable soup, apple pie and milk sent to him from the Automat. The actual time it takes him to eat this is one minute and twelve seconds.

In the summer he sits on a camp stool outside of his theater, the Eltinge, watching the audience enter.

A good script, he considers, is one that makes him forget his cigar has gone out.

During the rehearsals of *The Shanghai Gesture*, the cussing, hard-boiled Mr. Woods blushed and had the author tone down some of the lines.

Buttons are always missing from his overcoat.

Once considered producing Shaw's *Back to Methuselah*. This play takes three days for one showing. He rejected it saying: "I'm too nervous. I've got to know the next day if I've got a hit."

At the foot of his desk there is a cuspidor. He generally misses.

He is afraid of the dark. He sleeps with the lights on.

OUT of the mess of broken hearts, out of the string of speakeasies, out of the stage door, out of the glare of the White Lights, there has taken form a strange being. He is the soul of Broadway. He speaks its lingo. He symbolizes its credo. One little block, east or west of Broadway, and he is in another universe. Step up and shake hands with THE BROADWAYITE.

He considers it quite an honor if Madame Guinan bounces him over the head with a bottle.

After a two-minute acquaintanceship with anybody he calls the party by his first name.

His philosophy of life is merely a protective covering for his shortcomings. When he dies he still will be waiting for "the breaks."

He reads *Variety* from cover to cover. Can tell you where they got that inside story. Also, if it's true. Is certain his statement is the last word in the matter.

His manners are atrocious. He always keeps his hat on. Thinks it makes him look like a newspaper man.

He is a gag carrier.

Is a sidewalk critic. Stands on the curb during intermissions and gives lectures on the entertainment. Calls all the critics by their first names. He looks familiar to them.

When dining with anyone he orders filet mignon. And can outfumble anyone for the check. When eating alone he orders beans.

Remembers George White when he was only a hoofer. Recalls vividly how George followed his advice. Knows who really picks the girls for Ziegfeld. He informs everyone that Lillian Gish and George Jean Nathan really hold hands.

He talks loudly. Even when he whispers.

He has a repertoire of stories. Uses them again and again. Even employing the same gestures. He gets to be quite boring.

He is unfeeling. His proudest moment was when a chorine jumped from the ninth floor of a hotel because he jilted her. The newspapers spoiled it all by saying she fell.

Looks for his name in Ward Morehouse's recording of the celebrities present. Believes the list to be incomplete if his name is not included.

He thinks that dramatic criticism in this man's town is a matter of personal prejudice and that the Paramount Building is actually at the "crossroads of the world."

Had a sandwich named after him in a well-known delicatessen.

If given his choice to be anyone in all history he would select himself.

He has never been in the Metropolitan Opera House. Tried to crash it once. It was the Lambs' Gambol. He couldn't get by the ticket taker. He went in like a Lamb and came out like a lion.

Nothing has ever been known to embarrass him.

Will often reprimand a waiter in this manner: "How about a little service? Do you know who I am? I'm practically God."

Let him cough once. Then he believes that the night life has got him at last. That he has tuberculosis. A lozenge clears the throat and he is off again.

His ambition in life is to have his nameplate on a seat in the Chanin theaters.

He has written for almost every magazine in America. Has the rejection slips to prove it.

His favorite expression is "I told you so."

He is greatly admired by folks who don't know him.

It is utterly impossible for him to keep a secret.

He tries to be at his wittiest before charming females.

Is always telling columnists how to run their columns. When called upon to act as a guest columnist he strangely disappears. It was the first time he was off Broadway in years.

He can play bridge. When he does his partner

refers to the game as "The Bridge of Sighs."

He knows the "angel" for every show. He can prove that Irving Berlin doesn't write his own songs. He can't mind his own business.

It is rumored that he broke into show business by driving a truck for Cain's Theatrical Storehouse.

Is of the opinion that Jed Harris wears a beard like David Belasco wears a collar. Merely as a trademark.

His favorite indoor sport is getting "tight." Then he imagines he is God's Messenger, and that his mission in life is to lick the entire world, individually. They usually place him behind a piano until he regains consciousness.

He was once a Boy Scout.

He is always the life (and death) of the party.

He is the type of person who is probably reading this article now, thinking it is about a couple of other guys.

LYNN FONTANNE. She's just a bird in a "Guilded" cage.

Was born in London. Her name was Lily Louise Fontanne. Changed the Lily Louise to Lynn because it sounded better.

Every morning for breakfast she has honey and rolls.

She has a wide smile, a throaty laugh and a robust sense of humor.

Lives in a triplex apartment in East Thirty-sixth Street. The pride of the apartment is a fireplace with an aluminum background. The telephone operator there has a list of the people she will speak to.

A woman, above everything else, she believes, should be fashionable.

During the World War she worked in London as an emergency chauffeur.

She met Alfred Lunt, her husband, during a rehearsal of *Clarence*. Entering to speak his lines to her, he tripped and fell at her feet. It could be said that he fell for her. Later he suggested that they rehearse in the open air. He took her riding in an open carriage through the park. He gave their scripts to the driver to read while he proposed to her.

Dislikes short dresses and never wore them when they were the style. Wears a blue smock in her dressing room or when idling about the house.

She can foot pedal an Ampico piano longer and better than anyone in this state.

Avoids going to parties. Always giving the same excuse: "I'm too tired." An actress, she insists, should keep away from her public. She is fond of dancing but seldom does.

After the opening performance of *Strange Interlude* she slept for fifteen hours.

Her husband's pet name for her is "Rich Lynnie" because she is always saving her money.

Doesn't like tinned food and people who rub their hands together. Hates to wear stockings but does. Likes to wear jewelry but doesn't. Hates to write letters and seldom does.

When traveling she brightens up her hotel room with chintz curtains and window flowers which she buys at Woolworth's.

Her great ambition in life is to be a writer of critical essays.

Changes her perfume weekly. Claims a change of perfume is a change of attitude.

Two years ago, knowing that she was to be operated on for appendicitis, she played through an entire performance against doctor's orders. Her substitute wasn't ready. And she didn't want the show to miss a performance.

Other people call her husband by his nickname, "Bill." She always calls him Alfred.

She visited her home town, London, last summer for the first time in ten years. She went into a glove shop. The clerk greeted her with: "Oh, how do you do. So glad that you're back. You've been acting out in the colonies, haven't you?"

Her favorite dish is broiled scallops.

She changes her coiffure for every show.

Among the great English writers she knows personally are Shaw, Wells, Bennett and Kipling. Met Bernard Shaw and Mrs. Shaw last summer. Mrs. Shaw spoke to her about curtains. Bernard went in to trim his beard.

She likes all foods that aren't good for her. Her husband is always putting her on a diet.

Ellen Terry gave her her first lessons in acting. This consisted of winding a bed sheet around her with the train in front. Then she had to walk up and down the room until she could handle the train gracefully.

Of all the books ever written her favorite is Arnold Bennett's *Old Wives' Tales*.

Charlie Chaplin once mistook her apartment for a speakeasy. And her for the proprietor because she was so hospitable.

Costumes and makeup are as important to her as performances. Spends as much time perfecting these as she does rehearsing her part.

Men, she claims, should wear more gay colors.

Believes that no woman should ever be separated from her husband for more than a month. Her contract with the Guild provides that she and Mr. Lunt must always be playing in the same city —if not in the same play.

She loves to chat with taxi drivers. She learns things.

She hates to get dried after taking a bath.

GREETINGS

"JUST GREETINGS"

J. P. McEvoy. Two days after he was born this greeting card arrived:

(To Mrs. McEvoy On The Occasion of Her Son's Birth.)

I hear that Dame Fortune has been kindly
  And blessed you with a boy so fine
And given you something to be proud of
  In future years when you sit by a lonesome pine.

May he grow up to be healthy and sturdy
  And good to his mother and true,
And be loved by countless millions
  As he is loved by You.

His first piece of writing appeared in the South Bend *News*. He inserted a job-wanted advertisement.

For some unknown reason he is afraid to enter a laundry.

Lives at Woodstock, N. Y. Is the proud possessor of two blessed events and a St. Bernard dog. The two children are now attending school in California. The dog, dying of loneliness, is to be shipped there next week.

The only jewelry he wears is a black opal ring. Wears this because everyone says it is unlucky.

Is very fond of people who resemble him.

He saves unused return postal cards.

Never actually writes a play or story. He dictates everything. Always has two secretaries working. Never revises any of his manuscripts. *Show Girl* has fourteen chapters. It was dictated at fourteen sittings.

He is unable to part his hair.

Believes there should be a law against bed makers who never tuck in the sheets at the foot of the bed.

As far as comedians go he starts laughing if he's in the same city as Jimmy Durante.

Always buys two copies of a book. One to read and one to lend.

His full name is Joseph Patrick McEvoy. His mother named him Joseph. His father named him Patrick. Not caring for either, he became J. P. McEvoy.

He has a picture of his wife in every room.

Still receives royalties on some of the greeting cards he wrote. His favorite is the following:

> *Eve had no Xmas*
> *Neither did Adam.*
> *Never had socks,*
> *Nobody had 'em.*
> *Never got cards,*

Nobody did.
Take this and have it
On Adam, old kid.

He was once an amateur wrestler. Gave it up because he didn't like being on the floor.

He hates to see people in wet bathing suits.

His first book to be published was a volume of poetry titled *Slams of Life*. He has the names of those who bought it. Two more sales and he could have formed a club.

Smokes a cigar from the moment he turns off the shower in the morning until he puts on his pajamas at night.

His pet aversions are women's elbows, chocolate candy all melted together, fishing stories, fishermen, fish, Laugh, Clown, Laugh; radio talks on how to make hens lay, buying new shoes, mixed quartets, Laugh, Clown, Laugh; runs in silk stockings, three-piece orchestras, waiters who breathe down his neck and Laugh, Clown, Laugh.

When in New York he puts up at the Algonquin. If working on a story or play he and his wife occupy separate rooms.

His first writing for the stage was a vaudeville sketch. *Out of the Dark*, written with John V. A. Weaver. It played only two performances in a four-a-day vaudeville house.

His favorite composers are Tschaikovsky, and

Gershwin. His favorite conductors are Toscanini and Frank Kennedy of the Fifth Avenue bus line.

Has two mottoes. One for the home and one for the office. The motto hanging in his house is: "Let No Guilty Dollar Escape." The motto hanging in his office is: "Watch Your Hat and Coat."

Dislikes all the Hungarian Rhapsodies from number one to twelve.

His idea of a grand time is hearing Paul Robeson sing anything, going to Havana, being petted by any brunette not over five feet five, depositing royalty checks from Simon & Schuster, throwing pebbles into a lake, reading anything by James Stephens, eating kalteraufschnitt mit kartoffelsalat and attending a Chinese theater with a Chinaman.

He once got sick eating a sandwich that was named after him.

After he quit running a column in the Chicago *Tribune* the circulation of the *Tribune* dropped from forty thousand to a million.

AN author spends months writing a play. A producer stakes everything on it. Days and nights of weary rehearsals with stars sweating. The play opens. Evening dress and silk hats. Speculators selling tickets on the sidewalk. Everybody is so happy. A few months later a truck backs up at the stage door. The path of glory leads but to Cain's.

PATRICK CAIN is the owner of that theatrical storehouse. Everybody calls him Patsy.

He attended P. S. 32. Bows his head shamefully when admitting that he didn't have the honor of receiving a diploma.

His father, John J. Cain, a former policeman, started the trucking business forty-two years ago. He used to help his father just for the ride.

Seldom goes to an opening night. Producers, considering him a jinx, shoo him away. He has attended more closing nights than any other man in the world.

Has a broken nose. This he received in his youth during a block fight.

His warehouse is located at 530 West Forty-first Street. Directly opposite is an old brewery with a statue of a fallen man holding a schooner of beer. He seems to be saying to those shows entering their final resting place: "Here's to Better Days."

Is happily married and the proud possessor of four children. Has his own home in Flushing. It was built especially for him by a stage carpenter.

He doesn't drink, smoke or use profane language.

Rarely eats in restaurants. Has breakfast and dinner at home. Has lunch at his sister's, who lives two blocks from his place of business.

The storehouse consists of five stories and a basement.

The fifth floor is for the shows of Aarons and Freedley, Schwab and Mandel, Gene Buck and the personal belongings of W. C. Fields and Laurette Taylor. The fourth floor holds the last remains of Florenz Ziegfeld's *Follies* and George White's *Scandals*. Their mighty efforts for supremacy rest in peace. The third floor is for Sam H. Harris, Douglas Fairbanks, A. L. Erlanger and the Paramount Theatre. The second floor is occupied by Richard Herndon and others. The basement is for the canvas "drops." They are rolled neatly and lie row on row. Their tombstone is an identification tag on which is scrawled in pencil: "Garden Drop—Follies— 1917."

He drinks two chocolate ice cream sodas every day. On Sunday evenings he takes the entire family to the neighborhood drug store and treats them to sodas.

Employs only four men—a night watchman, a day watchman, a bookkeeper and a superintendent. He hasn't a secretary. But the superintendent, attired in greasy overalls, takes great pride in referring to himself as "Patsy's typewriter."

He hires his help by the day. Employs exactly the number he needs for that day's work. While on a job if the men eat before three o'clock they must pay for the meal. If they eat after three he must. Every day he phones his men at exactly one o'clock and says: "Boys, I think you ought to knock off now and get yourselves a bite to eat."

He has eight gold teeth in his mouth. They make him look dignified.

Reads only two things. They are the dramatic reviews and the cartoons in the *New Yorker*.

Has the same amount of strength in his right hand as he has in his left. He can write just as unintelligibly with both.

His name often occurs in theatrical reviews. One critic referred to a show as "A typical Cain success." Another said: "The audience was so bored and quiet you could hear Cain's trucks carting the show away after each act was over." The prize of them all was the one by Rennold Wolf. For his review of Arthur Hopkins's first production, *Steve*, Mr.

Wolf merely wrote: "A Voice From Cain's—I Gotcha, Steve."

Until three years ago he wore red flannel underwear. Now in the summer he wears balbriggan union suits and in the winter two-piece fleece-lined underwear.

He bought an automobile a year ago and is still learning how to drive it.

Nothing tickles his palate like a good plate of corn beef and cabbage—Irish style. Whenever the Cains have company for dinner they serve roast chicken. This he considers "living high."

Wallack's is his favorite theater. It is said that his horses stop there by force of habit.

His office is on the ground floor of the building. His desk is an old roll-top affair with hundreds of initials scratched on it. The drawers are filled with needles, sewing thread, penknives, old pen points, kodak photographs of his children and his house, screws, nails and holy pictures. The wall is decorated with a picture of his father, wooden cutouts of Dutch boys and girls and a large picture of an American flag with the caption "Ours" under it. To the left of his desk a policeman's nightstick stands handy. To the right is a pail of milk for the office cat.

He attends the eleven o'clock mass at St. Andrew's Church, Flushing, every Sunday—hot or cold.

Always tucks the ends of his tie inside his shirt.

When his father died he willed Patsy his favorite horse. According to the terms of the will, he must take the horse for a vacation every summer.

He doesn't do any advertising. But if he did, his slogan would be: "Not a Show in a Carload."

THE MARX BROTHERS. They are known as Groucho, Harpo, Chico and Zeppo. Their real names are Julius, Arthur (formerly Adolph), Milton and Herbert. They were given their nicknames by a kibitzer at a poker game in Galesburg, Ill.

They always sign their contracts in green ink.

Three of them are married, Harpo, the unmarried one, has been on the verge eight times. With eight different girls.

Have been known as "The Three Nightingales," "The Four Nightingales," "The Six Mascots" (in this act they were assisted by their mother and the other brother, Gummo, now in the cloak and suit business), and "The Four Marx Brothers." The name of the act depended on how many of the family were in it.

Are nephews of Al Shean of Gallagher and Shean fame.

Groucho's theatrical career started at the age of thirteen in a Gus Edwards "School days" act. He was fired in the middle of the tour because his voice changed.

Harpo's début was made twenty-two years ago

on a Coney Island stage. He was pushed on by his mother when "The Three Mascots" were playing there. He wore a white duck suit with a flower in his buttonhole. Frightened, he stood with his back to the audience and didn't say a word until the curtain fell. Has yet to speak a word on the stage. After his début "The Three Mascots" was changed to "The Four Nightingales."

After finishing a sandwich at a party, Groucho throws the plate out of the window.

Chico is the business member of the quartet. It was he who arranged for their first appearance in a Broadway show.

Harpo was once a bellboy at the Hotel Seville. He earned an extra twenty-five cents a week from Cissie Loftus for taking her dog for a daily stroll. Chico played the piano in nickelodeons. Groucho drove a grocery wagon in Cripple Creek, Col. He had a burning desire to become a prize fighter.

Whenever they want to get out of an engagement Harpo fakes an appendicitis.

Their dressing room is always filled with visitors. Herbert Swope, Neysa McMein, Harold Ross, Alexander Woollcott, Heywood Broun and Alice Duer Miller are nightly visitors when they have a show in town.

Chico will bet on anything. Merely say it is a nice day and he will say: "I'll bet you."

Harpo's and Zeppo's favorite dish is crab flakes

and spaghetti. Groucho and Chico, on the other plate, are especially fond of dill pickles and red caviar.

The four of them play the stock market. That's why they're still in the show business.

Whenever Groucho wants to visit his broker he tells his wife he is going to play golf. He visits his broker attired in a golf outfit, carrying a bag of clubs.

Are always playing practical jokes. Annoy interviewers by pretending they are slightly deaf. Another gag is Groucho telling their life story. He stops at a certain point saying: "This is all I remember of my life. Chico knows the rest." Chico continues with an entirely different story. He also stops in the middle, offers the same excuse, referring the interviewer to Zeppo, who continues the process until all four have told a different story of their lives.

Offstage Groucho, Chico and Zeppo occasionally wear glasses.

Zeppo is in the real estate business. He tries to sell property backstage.

Harpo is the best poker player of The Thanatopsis Club. Has won enough money from Heywood Broun to pay for young Heywood's tuition fee through any college in the country. Is also a great croquet player. Often plays in Central Park for a thousand dollars a game.

Their grandfather was a noted strolling German magician. Their grandmother was also in the act. She played the "accompanying music" on a harp.

They failed to click only once. In a London Music Hall. The Englishmen booed and threw pennies on the stage. Groucho stepped to the footlights and told them they were cheap. He dared them to throw shillings. They made more money at that performance than they were paid for the week.

To Harpo every woman, regardless of her name, is Mrs. Benson.

Harpo can play any musical instrument. Chico plays the piano and harp. Groucho plays the guitar. Zeppo likes to listen to the radio.

Groucho once owned an Airedale dog. The dog could only walk north. He traded it for four city lots in Salt Lake City. Later discovered that the lots were under water.

After he had been playing the harp for five years Harpo decided to take lessons. Shortly he was showing the teacher tricks on the harp. Suddenly he stopped taking lessons. He realized it was costing him $10 a week to teach the professor how to play.

Harpo is a friend of Bernard Shaw. The first time he met Shaw, Harpo was stark naked.

Before *Animal Crackers* opened Groucho told Sam Harris that he didn't think Zeppo would be with them; that there would be only three instead of the usual four in the show. Mr. Harris, rather indifferently, replied: "Oh, that's all right with me." Groucho replied: "But it isn't all right with us. We want more money."

Harpo has a passion for having his head scratched. The four of them like to have the soles of their feet tickled.

THE Woman Of It. GERTRUDE LAWRENCE.

She is always recognizing people she has never seen before.

Although fond of flowers and has plenty about the house she will never wear any.

Her father was a singer with a company of touring English minstrels. Her mother acted with the troupe. As a baby she was left in a clothes basket in the dressing room while they were onstage. At the age of four she sold programs in the theaters. Made her stage début when she was six, playing kid parts in England, Scotland and Ireland. Had cards printed reading: "Miss Gertie Lawrence, Child Actress and Toe-Dancer."

Has a small beauty mark, difficult to see, on the right side of her chin.

Is a good tennis player and an excellent swimmer. In the summer she goes to the beach, in a very business-like way, to acquire a heavy coat of tan.

She avoids wearing a hat whenever possible. Loathes clothes except when she has to dress up. At home she walks about attired in pajamas. When retiring for the evening she dons a nightgown.

Her most expensive habit is buying automobiles. She owns three.

Has a mania for clocks. Has twelve in her apartment. No two of them ever register the same time.

She first set foot in this country on Christmas eve, 1923, when the company of the first *Charlot Revue* arrived here. No one was present to greet her. She and Beatrice Lillie sat on their trunks on that lonely dock for an hour. They cried and sang Christmas carols.

When talking to a person who uses an accent, she can't help mimicking that person in conversation.

Her choice selections in foods are beef stew, kidney pudding, fruits out of season, greasy potato chips and ripe olives soaked in garlic. Buys things from pushcarts, like roasted chestnuts, and eats them while walking along the street.

Wears horn-rimmed glasses when she reads or wants to look dignified.

In *Candle Light* she played her first straight rôle in this country. In London she played the lead in *Icebound*. Over there she is also noted for her male impersonations.

She goes to fortune tellers and reads dream books, believing in them implicitly.

Her nicknames are "Squirrel," "Peaches" (this one annoys her), "G" and "Dormouse."

Lindbergh is her hero. In her press book, which contains every story and picture of her that ever appeared, she also has pasted the newspaper accounts of Lindbergh's flight, reception and marriage.

Her two favorite games are poker and backgammon. She attends every prize fight, bicycle race and ice hockey game that she can.

Likes to talk in a husky voice and welcomes a slight cold because it enables her to do this.

She can fix a fuse, if one blows out, or repair mechanical troubles. For years she had a tiny French telephone, the type banned by the telephone company. Wherever she traveled, London, Paris, New York, she took it with her and installed it herself.

Prefers definite shades of color in her clothes. She looks best in either black or white.

She is most comfortable when sitting on the floor—and generally does.

Of all her songs, her favorite is "Watch Over Me," from *Oh, Kay*. She takes a singing lesson every day and is now learning to sing in Italian.

Her secret ambition is to write a play. Every week she decides to become something else. Now she wants to be a sculptress. She bought some modeling clay, a smock, a book on how to make models life size in twelve easy lessons, and is now trying to do things.

Gets "black moods" and loves to be miserable. When feeling this way she runs records of "sad blue songs" on the gramophone for hours.

Her prize possession is a drawing of a pig. The artist is the Prince of Wales and he drew the picture while blindfolded.

There is nothing she does better or more often than sleep. She can take a nap any time, whether it be in a chair or a bed, dressed or undressed.

She has a daughter, Pamela Barbara May, aged eleven. The girl was named Pamela after a play popular in London at the time of her birth. Barbara after her father's sister, who is a nun. May after the month in which she was born.

She is most cheerful on rainy days.

When traveling she always carries her own silverware, eiderdown covers and bed linen with her. Thus uses her own equipment, whether stopping at a hotel or on board an ocean liner.

She likes to play with her toes.

HE is Mrs. Horowitz's little boy, Jacob. But in the bright lights of Broadway, it's JED HARRIS.

Four years ago he knew where the Automat was but he didn't have the nickel. Today he is worth over a million dollars. In the days when he didn't have a penny he told everybody he could make a fortune whenever he was ready.

He wears only the top part of his pajamas.

Was born in Vienna and came to this country at the age of three. He has three sisters and one brother.

His personal appearance is a minor thing with him. He has had the same hat since he's been in the show business. If it isn't the same hat it looks the same.

Is, however, particular about his shoes. They must always look like new. Every other week he purchases a new pair.

The script of *Broadway*, originally titled *Bright Lights*, was rejected by almost every theatrical manager. George M. Cohan turned it down because he didn't like the characters. William A. Brady because he couldn't get Texas Guinan to play the hostess. A. H. Woods refused, writing these noble words across the title page: "Not with my money, sweetheart." On a first reading even Jed Harris rejected it. Six months later, reading it for the second time, he bought it and became famous.

He carries very little money with him. Generally allows someone else to grab the check.

He hates to shave due to the fact that he has "tissue paper" skin. No matter how careful the barber is, his face always bleeds after a shave.

Seldom does he drink. He likes to pretend that he is drunk.

His ambition is to have his own ocean liner.

During rehearsals of a play he is a mad man. For the first couple of weeks he has no confidence in the script. After he has passed through that period he believes he has the greatest play in the world.

Every Friday evening he visits his parents and has noodle soup. They still live in the same house in Newark.

He plays the violin well and is quite adept at card tricks, which he learned from a vaudeville magician. At parties he entertains by reciting complete acts of his plays.

Does most of his work between midnight and four in the morning in the office.

His favorite meal is one consisting of beans, hash, pickles and near beer.

He was fired from the publicity job of a Jewish charity organization by a man who is now doing theatrical interviews for a leading metropolitan morning newspaper. He has issued a standing order that this man must never be permitted to interview him. He is careful, however, that this interviewer receives aisle seats for all of his shows.

With the money he made from *Love 'Em and Leave 'Em* he got married.

No matter who the author or the star is, if he doesn't like the play, he closes it out of town. He tried for two years to get Ina Claire to appear in a play for him. Then he closed that play, *The Gaoler's Wench,* forty-eight hours before it was due on Broadway.

He possesses the intuition of a woman.

Once he talked a college chum into taking him to Europe. Quarreled with the chap in Paris. After bumming about London he worked his way back to America in the stokehole of a boat.

He is afraid of old age.

His favorite photograph is the one in which he is sitting on a table with his hands carefully folded in his lap. His shoulders are rounded and his eyes have that faraway look—like a genius.

He can talk anybody into anything.

Works on the script of every play he produces. Always suggests new situations to be written into the play. Twenty-four hours later he telephones the playwright to inquire if the suggested bit has been written. If it hasn't he merely says: "If you'll do that you'll make me very happy" and hangs up.

Dreads the impact of cold water. Whenever he goes to the seashore he sits on the sand all day without going into the water.

He does everything in high gear. Worries about things. Delays doing them until he has worked himself into an emotional state. Then he is a tornado. Nothing can defeat him.

Lives in a duplex apartment in Sutton Place. His second ride in the elevator in that building cost him exactly $212.

Recently in a restaurant a waiter wishing to impress the people at his table pointed and said: "See that man. That's Jed Harris. He shaves and it comes right out again."

Noel Coward calls him "Destiny's Tot."

On the opening night of his plays he is home sleeping. Whenever he wishes to break an appointment or avoid a tense situation he goes to bed.

His favorite character in all history is Jed Harris.

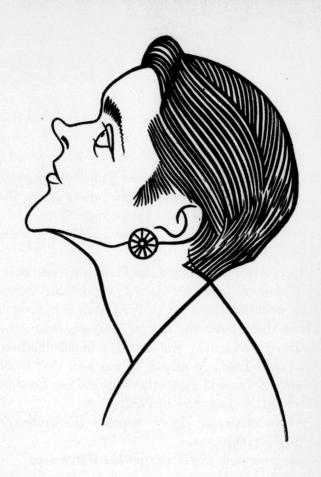

LITTLE EVA

Eva le Gallienne was born January 11, 1899, as the Bow bells of London were tolling seven. She is five feet four and weighs 128 pounds.

She can do anything with her left hand that she does with her right.

Her father is Richard Le Gallienne, the poet. Her mother, Julie Norregaard, a journalist. After they separated she went to Paris with her mother. Lived there until the age of thirteen, when she returned to London and enrolled in Sir Herbert Beerbohm Tree's Academy. It was here that Lyall Swete saw her and presently she made her London début in *The Laughter of Fools*.

At an affair she always requests the orchestra to play a tango.

She sews well. Loves to iron her shirtwaists.

Left England for America to play in *The Laughter of Fools* for David Belasco. After two weeks of rehearsals the play was shelved.

Likes very sheer stockings and suède shoes. Wears suède gloves, always making it a point to buy them a size too large.

Her first appearance on the American stage was

with Harrison Grey Fiske in *Mrs. Boltay's Daughter*. Richard Le Gallienne, who hadn't seen her since she was three, attended a performance. She had the rôle of a colored maid. Mr. Le Gallienne on seeing her exclaimed: "My God! Is that my daughter?"

She plays the piano, the guitar (gypsy and Spanish), the harp and the piccolo.

The members of her theatrical troupe call her "Saint Eva." On the opening night of a play she sends every woman in the company a box of flowers. Every man receives a gardenia.

Her suits are short, while her evening dresses sweep the floor.

Whenever she goes to the theater she insists upon sitting in the first row.

Seldom touches hard liquor. Her taste is for wines. Prefers French cooking to any other style and eats almost a basketful of fruit a day. She adores ripe figs.

When eleven years old she made a copy of Mme. Bernhardt's memoirs in longhand. It required two volumes and a year's labor. When Sarah Bernhardt heard of this she asked to see her and wrote a tribute on the flyleaf of the first volume. A copy of this now hangs in Miss Le Gallienne's dressing room.

Former President Coolidge selected her as, next to Lindbergh, the outstanding person of 1928.

Her favorite cultivated flower is the camellia. She loves to pick wild flowers.

Has a wonderful collection of antique jewelry. Always wears earrings. One of her choice possessions is a cross made of emeralds. She wears this dangling from a silver chain which girdles her black velvet evening gown.

She owns a car and operates it herself. She gets a big kick out of driving in traffic.

Always wears a Russian turban in winter and a velvet tam, gray or black, in summer. She has one large black felt hat that she wears when she's really going out. She has had the same Russian marmot coat for the past fourteen years. It has never been remodeled.

She admires Mrs. Fiske tremendously.

She likes long hair. Her own is bobbed because she has to wear a wig in almost every play. All her wigs are imported from France.

Show Boat she considers the best musical she ever saw. Is very fond of modern composers. Continually plays Gershwin's "Rhapsody in Blue" on the piano. Also plays the record of it.

The only sweet she reaches for is Martzepan. This is a candy made of almond paste.

She speaks, reads and writes English, French, German, Russian and Danish fluently. Converses in Spanish and Italian and knows enough Greek for use in reference work.

Her home is decorated with toy animal ornaments.

She has a direct telephone from her dressing room to her apartment. From her dressing room to the box office and from her apartment to the box office.

Is very proud of the fact that Mrs. Herbert Hoover visited her recently backstage.

Her two favorite colors are violet and blue. Always manages to wear something blue. The dressing rooms at the theater are painted blue. Her apartment is painted blue. Her personal stationery is blue. Her auto is blue. The color of her eyes is blue.

She is an expert fencer. Her teacher is always imploring her to desert the stage and take up fencing seriously. He honestly believes she could become the champion woman fencer of the world.

She is a member of the Girl Scouts of America.

Rudy Vallee was born July 28, 1901, in Island Pond, Vt.

His real name is Hubert Prior Vallee. Took the name of Rudy from Rudy Wiedoft, the saxophone player. His idol.

Curses like a stoker. Has a temper and when it is aroused he screams like a woman.

His father was a pharmacist and owned a drug store in Westbrook, Maine, until last summer. The father is a French Canadian. His mother is Irish. Has one sister, Kathleen Marie, and one brother, William, who goes to Fordham College and lives with him.

Doesn't drink much. When he does he takes a rye highball. The taste of Scotch makes him sick.

When the war broke out he ran away from home to enlist in the navy. While in a training school, they learned that he was only fifteen years old. He was put in the hoosegow until his parents called for him. Still thinks he was a sailor.

His boyhood ambition was to be a letter carrier.

Sleeps in gay-colored pajamas. He snores and grinds his teeth. Occasionally he has a hot-water bag in bed with him to keep his toes warm. Gets semi-nightmares and wanders in his sleep. Several times his brother pulled him back from walking out of a window.

Can play only two instruments. The saxophone and the clarinet. He two-fingers the piano a bit. He is left-handed.

As a kid and a student at Yale he was unpopular with the girls. While at college he majored in Spanish. His desire then was to be a wealthy South American business man.

He pinches the lobe of his ear with his finger nails when nervous.

Smokes occasionally. It is an English brand of cigarettes. He has posed for pictures smoking a pipe but detests one. Often requests people not to smoke a pipe in his presence.

The kind of a woman who appeals to him the most is one of the Lenore Ulric type of beauty.

Can often be seen eating in Childs' or in Thompson's one-armed lunch place. His favorite dish is buckwheat cakes with plenty of butter.

When playing at the Rendezvous, he sang so low that Gilda Gray told him "to go get a megaphone." He did. Now plans to use an all glass megaphone so people will be able to see his face when singing.

His blond eyebrows are not very prominent. Therefore for photographs and stage purposes he pencils in arched eyebrows.

Keeps all strings, bags and papers that he finds. His pockets are filled with bits of paper, cigarette crumbs, throat tablets and burnt matches. Buys every patent medicine that appears. He always carries at least three toothbrushes with him.

Whenever he takes a girl out to eat he tells her what to order.

Lets his clothes flop wherever he takes them off. Never bothers to hang them up. Is economical. Takes stains out of his suits with a home cleaning fluid.

While playing at the Paramount, two school-girls, watching him, decided that they had to meet him personally. Posing as interviewers from a high school paper, they were ushered into his dressing room. As a matter of courtesy, he offered his hand in greeting. One of the girls took it and fainted. The other fell back in a chair—exhausted. The house physician was called, and the girl was revived and escorted to the street. But not until the one who had clasped Rudy's hand let it be known that she was never going to wash the hand that touched her hero's hand.

His great ambition today is to make one million dollars.

When reading he prefers Western stories. Believes the greatest book ever written to be *The Guarded Heights*, a story of college life at Princeton, by Wadsworth Camp.

Of all the songs he sings his favorite is "Deep Night."

On May 11, 1928, he married Leonie Cauchois McCoy. The marriage was annulled the August of that year. He gives every girl the "Gray Dawn" test. Keeps them out until dawn, believing that if a girl looks good then she'll look good any time.

Has two scars on his body. One is from an appendicitis operation. The other is a bit of gravel in his left knee cap. The result of a motor-cycle accident.

The one thing in life he fears is that some day he will be fat and bald.

9 A. M. People who don't belong walking over a sleeping body. The lights are out and the sun is shining. Stores are opening for business and porters are cleaning out the theaters. Programs are swept aside. Last night's opening is now an old story. Working people are hurrying to their tasks. They're going to make money to spend when the lights flicker. Nobody along the Street thinking of amusement. They'll sell you insurance, a suit of clothes, a cup of coffee, but never a laugh. If Broadway were awake it wouldn't let these people on it. But the Street is only human. It must get some rest. There they go, not a real double-crosser, not a gangster, not an actor, not a guy hopped up with fake dreams. Merely real people. Walking up Broadway when it is asleep.

* * *

10:30 A. M. Broadway yawns. Actors in their sleep wake to rehearsals. Some poor nut has a song hit that no one will take off his hands. Ham and eggs at Childs'. Countless actors who believe that today their break may come. Press agents going to what they call work. Broadway yawns again. Part of it goes back to sleep. The other part marches. They don't make a dent. The Street still belongs to the foreign invasion. School kids and people out of work standing in line to get into the Paramount at the cheap morning prices. The afternoon papers begin to appear on the newsstands. Sounds of a jazz band practicing. It annoys the realtor two doors away. In a couple of weeks he'll pay to hear the same band and call it amusement. Dreary-eyed coryphées leaving side street hotels to hurry to rehearsals. The rouge and lipstick are the only thing genuine about them. They could put that on in their sleep. Don't you worry, they'll be repaid. Have their name in lights, get a husband, or else. Yawn, Broadway, but put your hand over your mouth.

*　　*　　*

2 P. M. Broadway is waking up. The light, the air, the sunshine is foreign. Matinée crowds now fill the streets. Actors are going to work. Why do they have matinées? You ought to see the same show some night that you saw in the afternoon. Where do people get the time to go to theaters in the afternoon? Why don't they sleep? Actors going to matinées. To see how they would have played the part or to applaud a fellow performer.

A night club has a rehearsal in the cellar. Work all night and work all day. It's a racket. Some people find heaven in a dive. Producers having their breakfasts. Big business deals written out on tableclothes. Do you know who's in town? Four guys are spilling the same exclusive inside story. Gray's is filled and Cain's is making room for another show. Broadway is waking up. Theatrical folks are hurrying to their doctors. To their dentists. To take a sun-ray bath. Must keep in good condition. What's the daytime for? The curtain's going up. More jazz bands are rehearsing. Someone just signed a big contract and is going to get his name in lights. What the hell good is daytime? You can't see your name in lights. Come on, Broadway, wake up. Get hot. Get dark.

*　　*　　*

7:30 P. M. It's getting dark on old Broadway. Its getting hot on old Broadway. Actors answering the 7:30 call of the theater. Grease paint. Bring in that latest shipment through the back door, will you? She's meeting him in front of the Rialto. It's an opening night down the street. Maybe they'll holler, "Author, author." He's invested everything in this one. Gee, I hope he clicks. He's a nice guy. The critics. I'd like to see one of them write a play. Bernard Shaw? I

mean a New York critic. Someone just cracked
a gag. Lights are flickering. Someone else just
cracked the same gag. Horns are tooting. Someone just had a reputation shattered. A new one
tomorrow. The sky is beautiful. In some part of
the world people are looking at the moon. It's
getting dark on old Broadway. It's getting hot
on old Broadway. No one can see above the
electric light. Loan it to me and I'll pay you
back tomorrow. I haven't got it myself. They're
all friends. All buddies. Just trying to do each
other a good turn if it will benefit themselves.
She's with another guy tonight. Don't know
how she can keep up the pace. There goes the
curtain. First nights. Glory seekers. Critics. Folks
in search of amusement. Panhandlers. Bums.
Noise. Lights. Greed. Backslapping. Tomorrow's
papers. What you're doing now doesn't count.
The present is of the past. Pretty important,
aren't you all? Ever walk through a graveyard?
All tombstones read alike. Broadway is getting
hot.

*   *   *

AFTER MIDNIGHT. Broadway is Broadway. Broadway is making whoopee. Prohibition is only for
the non-drinkers. Nobody knows what day it
is. Hey, waiter, this table! Policemen standing
in hallways. Long lines of cabs. We won't get

home 'til morning. Don't talk like that to him.
Want to get bumped off? Clubs banging on
tables. That's applause. Applause that's life to
an artist. I'm telling you it's a sure in the third
race at Havana tomorrow. Mr. Whoosis, I want
you to meet Miss Whatsis. Now I've got a scheme.
Some guys get all the luck. Broadway is making
whoopee. Evening dress and gorgeous gowns.
She was beautiful two hours ago. Legs. Arms.
Eyes. Desire. Fill it up again, I want to forget.
Tell me things, will you? I want to listen. Bad
music. Bad gin. Whirling bodies. Isn't this fun?
We're having a great time. I feel dizzy. It's
getting stuffy. You're not used to it. People who
are only eating sandwiches and drinking coffee
in plain restaurants. Talking dreams. Giving
the ego an outlet. A good listener is a good friend.
Stray lights in an office building. Strays walking up and down as if they were going places.
Couples window-shopping in dark windows. A
practically empty street car darting through the
night. Folks quarreling. Breaking their hearts.
Giving it to Broadway so it can be paved. The
street is practically deserted. But this is what
the hick in the stick believes is the real Broadway.
This is Broadway making whoopee.